CHANGING FORTUNES

Changing Fortunes

Industrial Sectors and Workers' Earnings

LEANN M. TIGGES

PRAEGER

New York
Westport, Connecticut
London

Library of Congress Cataloging-in-Publication Data

Tigges, Leann M.
   Changing fortunes.

   Bibliography: p.
   Includes index.
   1. Wages—United States. 2. Age and employment—
United States. 3. Industrial organization—
United States. 4. Social classes—United States.
I. Title.
HD4975.T5 1987   331.2'973   87-2357
ISBN 0-275-92580-3 (alk. paper)

Library of Congress Catalog Card Number: 87-2357
ISBN: 0-275-92580-3

First published in 1987

Praeger Publishers, One Madison Avenue, New York, NY 10010
A division of Greenwood Press, Inc.

Printed in the United States of America

The paper used in this book complies with the
Permanent Paper Standard issued by the National Information
Standards Organization (Z39.48-1984).

10   9   8   7   6   5   4   3   2   1

For Gary Paul Green,
my soul mate

Contents

Appendixes

Tables and Figures

TABLES

FIGURES

Preface

The election of Ronald Reagan was the most visible sign of the transformation of the U.S. political economy. During the recession in Reagan's first term, many other signs would appear. These were not totally new phenomena; rather they were the exaggeration of trends already firmly in place—decline in manufacturing, proliferation of women's jobs, weakening of organized labor, high unemployment, and increased international competition. Public frustration in the face of economic transformation found new forms of expression. Conservatism was on the rise. Social divisions grew as the fortunes of one industry or region seemed to come at the expense of another. In a new twist on an old theme, generational conflict emerged with the young voicing jealousy and anger over the advantages of the old.

At about the same time, in sociological journals a new perspective on social stratification was taking hold. The approach would come to be known as the *new structuralism*. This literature seemed to extol the virtues of monopoly capitalism by contrasting the relatively high earnings of workers in concentrated industries with the low earnings and limited mobility of workers in competitive industries. New structuralists seemed unaware of the trends begun in the 1970s; in any case, their concern with the economic outcomes of employment (stratification) generally neglected the dynamics of class struggle (social change) that produced the outcomes.

The intellectual origins of new structuralist thought in critical social science were forgotten as economic sector became just one more variable in the regression equation used to explain earnings or career moves. The term *economic segmentation* no longer conveyed its structural character; many sociologists would consider it an employment characteristic of individuals. The policy implications of these analyses could be turned into an argument for the creation of more jobs in the core sector of the economy. Few new structuralists would feel comfortable with such a probusiness conclusion.

Getting out of their intellectual corner seemed to require, not an abandonment of the new structuralist position, but a reformulation that would take into account the structural changes occurring in advanced capitalism. Toward that end, new structuralism must become a theory of social change and social stratification. Facilitating that development is a goal of this book.

I did not set out to develop a critique of new structuralism. Focusing on the situation of older workers, I was quickly drawn to new structuralist explanations of within-class inequality. Mass media accounts of generational conflict seemed to fit well with dual economy and dual labor market approaches to stratification. But I was troubled by incongruities between the major changes taking shape in the economy and the immutability of fortunes presented in new structuralist literature. I saw the insecurity offered by manual work, even in a union shop. It was an insecurity driven by forces beyond the control of individual workers—automation, relocation, international competition. But where were these forces in the new structuralist accounts? They were buried by the concern with consequences of structure; the idea of constraints had become a static one.

One way to direct concern within the new structuralist perspective back to the process of economic segmentation is to consider the changes occurring in the earnings determination process over time. My interest in the inequality associated with age has led me to ask a question much different from that posed in much of the new structuralist literature. I start by asking how the changes in the postwar economy have affected the position of age groups within economic sectors. I argue that age is more than a correlate of experience; it can also be seen as a correlate of power. Changes in the relative positions of age groups can reveal some of the changes in the resources available to various groups of workers. The transformations that influence the resources of workers include the rise of services and concomitant deindustrialization of the United States, the growth of international competition in the product and labor markets, the centralization of capital into fewer and fewer hands, and the proletarianization of the work force through advancement of bureaucratic and technical forms of control.

My findings indicate that workers' resources in the labor market are declining. Overall, the differences between the core and periphery sectors have diminished, and differences between the core transformative and core service industries have increased. Men in core transformative industries, a formerly advantaged group, experienced declines in the rate of return to age, and the advantage of core service employment diminished for older men. Economic sectors seem to mean little to women's earnings. For women, most jobs will be found in periphery service industries, and the rate of return associated with employment in this sector is much lower for women than for men.

The process of economic segmentation entails changes in the political economy of the United States. I believe that recent efforts to focus new structuralism on workplace organization will provide an important part of the picture of advanced capitalism. But we must be careful not to lose sight of the historical context of the larger forces that impinge on workers and their employers.

Acknowledgments

Early in my graduate career I shared an evening with two sociologists whose careers had begun almost at the same time as the discipline was forming in the United States. The sociologists were my (soon-to-be-retired) advisor, Donald O. Cowgill, and his (long-retired) advisor, Stuart A. Queen. I realized then that my intellectual debts extended back through generations of sociologists. Few among the rising generations will have such an opportunity to see their heritage and wonder at the changes and the constancy of the discipline.

Don Cowgill's contribution to this book began long before the idea for the research was developed. I learned a great deal from Don; he was an important professional role model, sage advisor, and special friend. Craig Jenkins brought his considerable breadth of knowledge and enthusiasm for ideas to the inception and revisions of this research project. My interaction with historian Jackson Lears continually renewed my skepticism about late capitalism and patent theories. He has contributed much to my development as a sociologist.

The preparation of this manuscript occurred while I was a postdoctoral fellow at the Carolina Population Center at the University of North Carolina at Chapel Hill. The Population Center provided a marvelous working and learning environment. The entire technical support staff richly deserves my deepest gratitude. Special thanks to Catheryn Brandon and Chanya Harris for their professional job of typing the many versions of the manuscript. David Claris did a beautiful job with the figures. Lynn Igoe, in-house editor, was incredibly efficient, thorough, and cheerful. The comments of Rachel Rosenfeld, my faculty preceptor, helped refine the arguments and analyses presented in this book. Intellectual and emotional support also came from Elizabeth Hervey Stephen. Her responses were always above and beyond the call of duty; her friendship refreshed me daily.

Finally, I want to thank Gary Paul Green, for whom my words of thanks will be woefully inadequate. Gary has challenged and encouraged me since our first semester as graduate students. His enthusiasm for learning, intellectual rigor, keen wit, remarkable memory, and enviable sense of humor have sustained me through times of lost faith. He has read and commented on all major versions of this manuscript and has heard about every idea that fizzled out before it hit print. He has helped me clarify my thinking and explore the implications of my thoughts. This book is largely the product of our daily discussions about our world.

1
The Problem of Conflict and Change

AN UNEASINESS

By 1981, the tension was apparent. The years of plenty seemed gone forever. The economy was stagnant. Joblessness was approaching levels not seen since the Great Depression. Surfacing again and again in editorials and newsmagazine articles were images of profound conflict in U.S. society, a conflict described not in terms of aggression but of animosity, a conflict of interests more profound, according to some, than that between management and labor (Drucker 1982). The conflict was between the older and younger generations. The theme sounds familiar to those who remember the social unrest of the 1960s and early 1970s, when Jerry Rubin declared that no one over thirty should be trusted. But the nature of the new tension was extremely different. This time the conflict was conservative, not reformist; it was over the established rewards of economic life, not over social values.

The increase in generational conflict is often viewed as a consequence of change in U.S. social structure. Like the nature of the conflict, the nature of the change is unclear. The conflict is attributed to the interference of the welfare state, economic stagnation, or high inflation and interest rates. Some would undoubtedly take all of these as symptoms of the same malady—advanced capitalism—and still others would see them as only part of the temporary disequilibrium brought on by the changing nature of technology. Whatever the reason, the U.S. economy seemed incapable of providing benefits to all members of society. One group's gain would be another's loss.

The Old Age Burden

The older generation was often portrayed as the villain, the younger as the victim. According to some who vocalized the tension, retirees are a burden on the young, a burden calculable by a simple economic formula: "The total burden of the elderly is the sum of goods and services they use minus the goods and services they produce" (Davis and van den Oever 1981, p. 14). The aged constitute a cost to the working population, a cost exacerbated by economic conditions. In a stagnant economy, social life becomes a zero sum game. The gains made by the politically powerful elderly are losses to the young who must support them in a time of slow growth in productivity.

Put bluntly, the old have come to insist that the young not only hold them harmless for their past profligacy, but sacrifice their own prosperity to pay for it. And the beauty of it all, at least for the old, is that so far the young have muttered barely a word of protest. (Longman 1982, p. 24)

But the anger was not directed solely at retirees; older workers were also the target. In a stagnant economy, growth of new jobs is slow. Since the young do not have enough new positions available to them, they seek positions occupied by older workers. The high incomes of older workers added insult to injury as the young found their buying power limited by high interest rates on inflated prices.

Those enraged by the declining opportunities available to the young were quick to cite statistics pointing to the widening generational inequality of the 1970s. The average real incomes of the young fell 12 percent in that decade, while median annual incomes of those over fifty-five years old rose over a thousand constant dollars. As the gap between the wages of younger and older workers widened, the share of the national income controlled by those over fifty-five increased from 24 percent in 1970 to 27 percent in 1981 (Fromson 1983).

Those who talked of the old age burden were adamant in demanding national policies that would lighten the tax burden on the young, a demand that entails reductions in entitlement programs for the old, particularly in Social Security. Davis and van den Oever (1981, p. 15), for example, argued that one important reason for women's entry into the labor market was the rapid growth in taxation, "of which a substantial part is for the aged." Lessening the old age burden would reduce the need for female labor force participation, thereby decreasing the supply of workers and presumably improving wages. Appalled by two-tiered union contracts that protect wages of current employees by sacrificing wages of the "unborn" (those hired after the labor agreement is signed), many young people proposed cuts in wages of older unionized workers whose pay increases have been greater than their gains in productivity (Fromson 1983).

Recovery and the Zero Sum Game

By 1986, the generational advantages had shifted, though none of the specific state policies favoring the young had been adopted. The worldwide recession and substantial drop in oil prices, along with the monetary policies of the Reagan administration, created a situation that appeased young workers. (The reference to young *workers* is important. Those who failed to find employment or lost their jobs in the Reagan years found little comfort in the administration's policies.) Interest and inflation rates were at their lowest levels in a decade. The economy was no longer stagnant, but the zero sum nature of economic life continued. The benefits of economic growth were not trickling down to most of the population; their shares of total income and wealth were lower than at any time since the end of World War II (U.S. Bureau of the Census 1985; *In These Times* 1986). This time the old appeared to be the losers.

Even relatively good economic times create problems for the elderly. With inflation at about 3 percent for the economy as a whole in mid–1986, retirees faced higher rates of increase in the very areas of greatest need—medication, insurance, nursing home and hospitalization costs, and utilities. Changes in Medicare and the insurance industry increased the amounts individuals must pay for medical care, while declining interest rates reduced retirees' incomes from lifetime savings (Geewax 1986). Since the level of overall inflation did not come up to the threshold level of 3 percent required to activate automatic cost-of-living adjustments in monthly Social Security checks, many older people's incomes were completely stagnant.

The lower prices of the 1980s had ramifications for workers, too. Unable to raise prices because of foreign competition, large manufacturing companies looked for ways to cut their costs. Strategies included obtaining concessions from workers, selling in specialized markets (such as designer goods), holding down inventories, and modernizing operations. Suppliers felt the pinch as their manufacturing customers demanded quicker delivery of goods for immediate production needs. Production operations of suppliers became smaller and less economical (Gordon 1985). Thus, even during economic recovery, manufacturing industries failed to produce jobs. In the recovery of the mid–1980s, 80 percent of jobs created were in services.

Unfortunately, many of these jobs cannot be considered good jobs. They are low and semiskilled service jobs, and not the professional and technical occupations that were to be the hallmark of postindustrial society. In the private sector, hourly wages in services are 11 percent lower than in manufacturing. The average hourly wage in services, adjusted for inflation, was actually lower in 1986 than ten years earlier (*Business Week* 1986). Of the projected 20 million new jobs likely in the 1980s, 15.4 million are expected to be in the services. The big gains are expected in areas not requiring a college education—secretary, nurse's aide, janitor, and sales worker. Fifteen million college graduates are expected to enter the labor force in this decade, but only twelve to thirteen million are thought to be needed (English and DeLouise 1983).

The perpetual swings of the economy, from recession to recovery and back again, seem to change the winners and losers in society. However, there are indications that recently the benefits of economic recovery are going to fewer and fewer participants in the game. More is involved than change in the business cycle.

INEQUALITY AND STRUCTURAL CHANGE

Changes in the structure of contemporary U.S. society appear to have an influence on the degree of inequality. Some of these changes are demographic. The entry of the baby-boom generation into the work force in the 1960s and 1970s was accompanied by a substantial twist in earnings associated with age—against the young. The lower earning power of young (twenty- to thirty-four-year old) male workers was especially evident for college graduates. Economists argued that the large size of the baby-boom birth cohorts and their high educational levels created an oversupply of skilled but inexperienced workers. This influx of educated workers increased the value attached to experience in skilled occupations, thus the twist in earnings (Freeman 1979; Welch 1979). The long-term consequences for the earnings of the baby-boom generation are unclear. Freeman argues that some permanent effect of cohort size on lifetime earnings is likely, though Welch predicts baby-boomers will be able to make up for lost earnings during future periods of labor shortage.

Cohort size has been shown to have an influence on men's earnings. However, strict attention to this factor has obscured an important aspect of economic inequality, that occurring within generations. Earnings inequality increased among males in every education and experience category during the 1960s and 1970s, and more men in every category earned no income over a full year (Dooley and Gottschalk 1982). Forces other than population age structure are at work; within the economy, the decline of manufacturing and growth of service employment are partly responsible.

Industrial Change and Burden of Age

Manufacturing has changed in location and capital intensity. Decline in the industrial states of the upper Midwest has produced a Rust Belt. There the loss of jobs occurred not only because of plant closings but also because of automation within plants. The automobile industry provides a good example of some of the changes experienced by the backbone of the U.S. economy.

Between 1978 and 1985, automobile jobs with Detroit's Big Three (Ford, General Motors, and Chrysler) dwindled from 770,370 to 551,941. Workers lucky enough to keep their jobs averaged fourteen months of layoff. Automation in the automobile sector is expected to displace an additional 50,000 workers by 1990. The modernizing factories will place increased emphasis on retraining. At a new General Motors plant in Detroit, 260 robots are in use, and $40 million is budgeted for training. The three-week mandatory training course for line workers seeks to develop skills in areas as diverse as robotics principles, mechanical principles, team building, and management principles (Reuters News Service 1986). Workers in the factories of the future will be under intense pressure to be partners with management—with the emphasis on cooperation, not decision making.

How older workers fare when manufacturing modernizes is suggested by studies on displaced workers dating back to the early 1960s. Wilcock and Franke (1963) use case studies of plant closings to conclude that displaced older manual workers were likely to be reemployed at lower wages than before, in service industries and small firms, and in jobs that seldom used past skills. Furthermore, employment prospects of older workers were unrelated to education levels. A more systematic study of dislocated workers in the 1980s revealed that little had changed; the younger the workers, the more likely they were to have found jobs after displacement (Flaim and Sehgal 1985, p. 6).

A special study conducted by the Bureau of Labor Statistics for the House Select Committee on Aging found the recession of 1982 particularly harmful to older workers. Between January and August of that year, the unemployment rate for older workers jumped 24 percent, compared with a 16 percent increase for the total work force. Those workers fifty-five and older were three times are likely as younger workers to give up the search for work, joining the ranks of the uncounted unemployed, the discouraged workers. The average length of unemployment for older workers, nineteen weeks, was 23 percent longer than for younger workers. The financial impact of long-term unemployment weighs heavily against older workers; many still have children at home or in college who must be supported. But reentry into the work force brings cuts in pay and in job status (Pepper 1982).

Older workers are vulnerable when factories modernize, as well as when they close. The desire of firms to recoup the costs of training discourages the retraining of older workers. The term *redundancy*, used by Europeans to denote permanent layoff, aptly describes the feeling of older workers. In testimony before the House Select Committee on Aging in 1982, older white- and blue-collar workers expressed their frustrations. A sixty-one-year-old former production manager told the politicians:

It may seem odd that I talk about a company that I worked for six years ago. Well, Mr. Chairman, it was during that year that the company had serious problems, and in order to salvage the operation, Teletron fired me and several other high-paid staff. My job hunt began then, and it has not stopped for a single day since. . . . After the unemployment checks ran out, after going through most of our savings, I was so depressed that I even considered suicide. (U.S. Congress 1982, p. 26)

A fifty-six-year-old machinist testified that he was first laid off when his employer sold the division in which he had worked thirty-eight years. He gained employment in another of the company's plants but lost his seniority.

As a result, when the second plant began to face financial problems I was laid off again. That was 6 months ago. . . . I have had a lot of time to think about my problems in the last six months, and I have just about decided that I should probably take some training in a new field. . . . But before I put out the money for training I want to be sure there will be jobs out there for an older worker like me when I finish. I cannot afford to waste time or money at this stage in my life. (pp. 23–24)

The only option available to many older men appears to be early retirement. Since 1960, labor force participation of men fifty-five to sixty-four years old has decreased substantially; at least part of this tendency toward early retirement can be attributed to older men's vulnerability to the business cycle (Clark, Kreps, and Spengler 1978; Rosenfeld and Brown 1979). Also contributing to older men's higher rates of nonparticipation in the labor force are "golden handshakes" and "open windows"—voluntary early-retirement incentive plans usually aimed at people over fifty with at least ten years of service to the company (Alsop 1984). The incentives typically include some combination of pension bonuses, medical-insurance benefits, and severance payments based on salary and tenure at the company. Many senior workers in firms such as Sears Roebuck and Company, Eastman Kodak Company, and American Telephone and Telegraph Company opted for the early retirement plans offered by their employers. Unfortunately, some came to regret their decisions when they found it more difficult to live on their pensions than they had anticipated; others disputed the voluntary nature of the plan. A U.S. district court ordered Chrysler Corporation to rehire eight of its workers who were forced to choose between early retirement and layoff (Pepper 1982).

Older women face the greatest problems. When displaced from their jobs, they are less likely than men to be reemployed (Flaim and Sehgal 1985), and in retirement, older women are less likely than men to receive pensions. In 1984 only 20 percent of women 65 and older received pensions, compared with 43 percent of men that age. Furthermore, the size of women's pensions was only about half that of men's (Williams 1986). The low salaries and discontinuous work patterns of women contribute to their financially depressed life in old age.

The Service Economy

With the decline in manufacturing, many hung their hopes on the rise of service industries in the information age. The optimism of social scientists and politicians faded when confronted with the harsh realities of service-sector employment in the 1980s. The shift to services appears to have negative consequences for social groups who had made substantial gains in the late 1960s and early 1970s. Nonwhites, in particular, find it difficult to get jobs in many service industries (Stanback and Noyelle 1982). (The negative effects of the changing U.S. industrial structure on nonwhites are also apparent in plant closings and relocations. Squires [1984] reports lowered minority employment in firms relocating from Illinois to the South and from central city to suburban locations.)

Growth in service employment is expected to be greatest in low-paying, sex-segregated jobs; for example, the top gainer through 1995 should be cashiers, whose wages are less than 60 percent of the national average (*Business Week* 1986, p. 80). Expansion of services has generated employment opportunities for women, but many opportunities are for minimum-wage, part-time, or part-year work. Of part-time workers who would rather have full-time employment, women outnumber men (U.S. Department of Labor 1980). In addition, in 1986 18 percent of women worked at the minimum wage, compared with 8 percent of men. Year-round, full-time minimum-wage employment could not lift a two-person family above the official poverty line (Pearce 1986, p. 2).

Few jobs in the service sector provide middle-level earnings. This has consequences for the economy and the society. Low earnings in services limit demand for goods and services, keeping economic growth slow. Social divisions between the bottom and top segments of the population are bound to grow with economic disparity. The trends are clear. According to a report by the U.S. Bureau of the Census (1985), the poorest two-fifths of all U.S. families received 15.7 percent of total national income in 1984, the lowest percentage since the information began to be gathered in 1947. The middle fifth received 17 percent of total income, also the lowest percentage since 1947. Not only are the poor getting relatively poorer, so are those in the middle. The reduction of income shares for the bottom three-fifths of U.S. families should alert social scientists to the structural changes in the economy that have facilitated this process. Of course, factors other than industry and occupation shifts—notably income redistribution policies of the government (taxes and welfare), organized labor's strength, monetary policies, and strength of the dollar—influence the distribution of income (and wealth) in the United States.

THE CONNECTION BETWEEN THE PERSONAL AND THE PUBLIC

In *The Sociological Imagination*, Mills (1959) challenged social scientists to make clear the elements of contemporary uneasiness. The uneasiness expressed above centers on the distribution of economic returns from labor force participation. The nature of economic life has given people the feeling that they are participants in a zero sum game, but they are unsure of the rules and have contradictory visions of the winners and losers. Unraveling the mystery depends on understanding the connection between personal trouble and public issue, between biography and history. The emphasis on generational conflict comes out of a one-sided view, that of personal troubles faced by participants in the struggle for rewards. What is missing is an understanding of the historical context of the struggle.

The types of personal troubles involved have been conveyed by the mass-media images of unemployed industrial workers and underemployed college graduates, of white-collar workers eager to climb a nonexistent corporate ladder, and of unionized workers threatened by corporate moves and the willingness of nonunion workers to work for lower wages.

As we have seen, the formulation and understanding of the public issue has been much less clear. Attempts to grapple with the historical transformation at the root of increased generational conflict have focused primarily on technological shifts in production. Technology has advanced, reducing the demand for the types of labor most available.

Technology is perceived as an actor in social life. It has its own dynamic, which humans are basically powerless to resist. Technology goes marching on; people must respond. Reskilling is the appropriate response. To the extent that policies are involved, the problem is viewed as one of overexpansion of the welfare state, its interference in the economy via retirement policies, and its failure to produce a labor force with appropriate skills.

Mills stressed that neither biography nor history can be understood without understanding both. Understanding the nature of recent social transformations is necessary if we are to gain an understanding of the changes in the structure of inequality. The discussion of generational conflict reveals that the nature of the threat perceived by individuals has not been clearly identified; the view of history that has accompanied such essays is also suspect.

In the coming chapters I review two sociological perspectives that focus on the relationship between societal changes and economic inequality—the technical functional view and the new structuralist approaches. Each perspective on social change leads us to expect certain outcomes for workers in the 1980s. Each view is weak in that it neglects the historical contingencies of organization that provide resources for class actors. I argue that changes in the distribution of economic rewards by age provide insights into the changing resources for workers in the class struggle. Instead of narrowly interpreting age as an indicator of work experience, I see it more broadly as a correlate of worker power. I thus hope to provide insights into the nature of the uneasiness, to link the personal troubles and public issues of advanced capitalism.

THE PLAN OF THE BOOK

My examination of age in the segmented economy begins with a discussion of a common theoretical approach to understanding the position of age groups, that is, the functionalist theories of industrial and postindustrial societies. My goal in chapter 2 is to show the connection between theories of stratification and societal change by focusing on the centrality of technology and market relations to these theories. Technological changes in production demand new occupational skills, and the filling of occupational roles is a key component of the stratification system, with rewards being allocated according to principles of supply and demand. In my review of status attainment theory, the functionalist theory of age stratification, and human capital theory, I draw the implications of these approaches for the position of older workers.

In contrast to the emphasis of technical functional theories on *what* is produced, new structuralist theories focus on *how* production is organized. In chapter 3, I link Marxian notions of social change to the variety of new structuralist theories of stratification—class, labor market, and economic segmentation approaches. I argue that the basic compatibility of Marxist and new structuralist approaches lies in their common emphases on power and access to resources. From this perspective, age is important in studies of stratification and social change because it can be viewed as a correlate of worker power within economic sectors.

But power is not a static quality; it is part of the dynamic of capitalism, class struggle. In chapter 4, I argue that a major flaw of new structuralism has been its neglect of the dynamics of segmentation and of changing resources of class actors. Despite the strengths of new structuralist stratification research, new structuralism has failed as a theory of social change. This failure is partially the result of new structuralists' exclusive focus on the organization of production and their consequent neglect of the type of production activity. To redress these failings, I review several of the important changes in the post–World War II U.S. economy and their effects on class resources in various production settings. Focusing specifically on industrial concentration, managerial control, worker skill, and capital mobility, I argue that one consequence of these changes is a weakening of the advantage of core-sector employment for workers in general and specifically for those age groups that had benefited most from it, the young and the old.

My approach to analyzing the changing position of age groups in the postwar United States is the subject of chapter 5. I discuss the data sources, time frame, and methodological decisions regarding independent and dependent variables in the analyses. I devote most of the chapter to a discussion of the virtues of an industry-level model of economic segmentation for the study of changing resources. I argue that a four-sector model that differentiates transformative and service industries of the core and periphery captures better the complexity of the what and the how of production than do capital sector models. (The term *capital sector* refers here to the variety of economic segmentation models that focus on the way production is organized. These models develop categories defined at least partially by industrial concentration.)

In chapter 6, I present the results of the analyses of age, segmentation, and earnings. The data support my argument that the changes in the U.S. economy since 1960 have affected the resources of class actors, strengthening the advantages of capital and weakening the position of workers. The trend toward greater employment in services (especially periphery services) does not offer the potential for good pay or job mobility to most workers, but within core transformative industries, the rules of the game also seem to be changing. New structuralists must consider the transformations in production as an ongoing process, rather than regard segmentation as a static characteristic of employment.

Returning to the themes of generational conflict and structural change in chapter 7, I explore the implications of my findings. I argue that

individualistic approaches cannot solve the problems of economic inequality in late capitalism. The connection between the personal troubles
and public issues of age inequality involves a shifting of resources away
from workers' influence. The zero sum game does not set the interests of
one generation against another; their interests are shared more than they
realize.

2
Transformation: The View from Academic Sociology

The transformation of societies has been conceptualized primarily in terms of changes in production and the labor process, but there is a lack of agreement on which features of production are the most important contextual ones for social inequality. Ideas about the character of societal transformation can be divided into two main camps: technological theories of academic sociology and new structuralist theories of critical sociology. Technological theories tend to define stages of societal change in terms of the dominant production activities, that is, the production of food, goods, or services. Technological changes accompanying product changes are determining features of social structure. "The essential difference between modern and traditional society . . . lies in the greater control which modern man has over his natural and social environment. This control, in turn, is based on the expansion of scientific and techno-logical knowledge" (Huntington 1976, p. 28). The processes of specialization and differentiation in production extend to the occupational sphere. As new occupations proliferate, the filling of positions depends increasingly on education and training, the mechanisms by which individuals develop technologically relevant skills. Economic rewards associated with occupations are distributed according to market principles of supply and demand.

The structural perspective on social change, on the other hand, is primarily concerned with shifts in patterns of ownership and control in production and with the accompanying class struggle. The technological features of production change, but these changes are not inevitable or completely determining. These changes result from decisions of those who own and control the means of production. Power, not skill, determines position in society. Whereas skill is an individual attribute, power is a group attribute. Economic returns to powerful groups are defined by production relations first and foremost, not market relations.

In this chapter, I explore the theories of social change and stratification in mainstream sociology. Because of the importance of technology to these theories, I refer to this approach as the *technical functional perspective*.

INDUSTRIAL SHIFT: TECHNOLOGY DRIVES CAPITALISM

Industrial Revolutions

In academic sociology, the term *development* is used to describe the processes that move a given society from traditional forms of organization to modern ones. The assumptions guiding the technical functional view of academic sociology are "(a) that the characteristic nature of any given society is primarily governed by its level of technological or economic development; (b) that consequently the most economically developed society (however that might be defined), at any given point of time, presents other societies with an image of their future in the present" (Giddens 1975, p. 19). This emphasis on the technical in development is matched by an emphasis on the functional in filling roles in each type of society. Inequality in the outcomes of the labor process tends to be explained by the possession of skills required to fill the functionally important positions in society. Societal development changes the skills in demand and also determines which individuals in society are likely to supply the needed skills.

The functional theory of stratification formulated in the 1940s (see Davis and Moore 1945; and Parsons 1940) provided the ground work for the theories of modernization and industrialization that dominated social thought in the 1950s and 1960s. Modernization theory is concerned with the transformation of societies from traditional forms with an agricultural base to modern forms with an industrial productive base. Although modernization is not synonymous with industrialization, the two processes are closely linked. *Industrialization* refers to economic development through a transformation of the sources and quantities of energy employed, from man and animal power typical of agrarian society to fossil fuels and other inanimate sources of energy (Lauer 1977). Industrialization is seen as essential to helping a society achieve the self-sustaining growth needed to take off into modernization (Rostow 1960). *Modernization* refers to the societywide transformation of economic, cultural, political, and social forms of organization from simple, traditional forms to highly complex, socially differentiated, functionally interdependent modern forms.

Changes in the economic organization of developing societies that accompany and result from industrialization (one form of modernization) include (1) substantial reduction in the proportion of the population directly engaged in agriculture, (2) shortage of skilled workers, (3) long-term upgrading of minimum and average levels of skill required, (4) increased demand for highly trained professionals, and (5) an eventual rise in the proportion of consumer expenditures allocated to services (Moore 1963). Social structural changes include a change in family organization from extended to nuclear, a weakening of informal social controls, and an increase in status inconsistency because of the variable relationship of income to other bases of stratification.

As a society industrializes, the division of labor becomes increasingly complex and the numbers of specialists grow. Work becomes the means to an end, rather than an intrinsically satisfying activity. Rewards available for distribution increase and the basis for their distribution becomes somewhat more equitable (Tumin 1960). Economic growth requires a fairly high degree of individual mobility and a placement system grounded on achievement. Labor as an institution must be both geographically and socially mobile, and property must be transferable. Organization takes a bureaucratic form, and motivation demands participation rather than passive adjustment (Moore 1963).

The origin of these changes is often attributed to the level of science and technology characterizing industrial society. Science and technology generate continual, rapid, widespread changes in production methods and products, changes that in turn create frequent changes in skills, responsibilities, and occupations of the work force (Kerr et al. 1960). Differentiation according to skill and executive responsibility below the level of top management is a function of the increasing size of the organization and the increasing complexity of technology (Parsons 1960). The result is a workplace with a wide variety of skills, responsibilities, and working conditions, requiring a hierarchical organization within enterprises. Levels of authority and specialization within the hierarchy carry with them a related differentiation according to compensation. Blau and his coauthors (1976, p. 20) provide an assessment of the central role of technology in societal change:

Few would question the impact of technology on society. Technological developments have caused the movement of people from farms to cities and from industrial to service occupations. They have stimulated the evolution of the modern economic organization, altered class structures, and affected political institutions.

The Postindustrial Revolution

Although theories of modernization and industrialization are still being applied to the Third World, concern with social change in advanced societies has led to the formulation of various theories of postindustrial society. Most influential in this area is the work of Bell (1976), who concentrates on the influence of technology in shaping society.

Broadly speaking, if industrial society is based on machine technology, post-industrial society is shaped by an intellectual technology. And if capital and labor are the major structural features of industrial society, information and knowledge are those of the post-industrial society. (p. xiii)

The major dimensions of a postindustrial society are the centrality of theoretical knowledge and the expansion of the service sector at the expense of the manufacturing sector. Important for postindustrial society is growth of services, since this represents the expansion of a new intelligentsia—those in health, education, research, and government. Instead of industrial workers, those in professional and technical occupations dominate the labor force. The public sector becomes the major area of employment and working with people becomes more important than working with things.

Although agricultural and industrial societies also have a service sector in their economic structures, the types of services found in those societies differ from those of the postindustrial society. In agricultural societies, most of the labor force is involved in agricultural pursuits, and those in the service sector tend to provide personal services. Industrial societies, with the majority of the labor force in semiskilled occupations, also have a large service sector, but the types of services provided aid industrial production; particularly important are transportation and distribution services. Within the service sector of the postindustrial society, professional and technical occupations are very important, especially those involving health, education, research, and government. The work of Singelmann (1978) verifies this historical shift of employment within the service sector for seven advanced countries.

Summary

Technical functional theories of industrial and postindustrial development emphasize the determining role of technology in social organization. Stages of development are defined by the dominant form of technology used in production—animal in preindustrial, machine in industrial, and intellectual in postindustrial society. Societies progress from one stage of social organization to another according to their abilities to develop and use new technologies. The evolutionary character of social change means that other aspects of society respond to the changes in production, and new systems of prestige and power are developed. In the following sections, I discuss the theories of stratification inherent in these technological theories of social change.

STATUS SHIFT: OCCUPATIONS AND EARNINGS

The development of society from one type of production system to another has long been seen to have consequences for social stratification. The evolutionary social theorists of the late nineteenth century, Maine, Tönnies, and Weber, expected greater equality as societies became larger and more complex. Theories of industrial development and modernization describe similar beneficial changes for societies as they move from an agricultural base to an industrial one. Distinguishing characteristics include changes from predominance of patterns of ascription and particularism to norms of achievement and universalism, from stability of groups and limited spatial mobility to a high degree of social and geographic mobility, from simple and stable occupational differentiation to a well-developed occupational system, and from a deferential stratification system to an egalitarian class system with a prevalence of functionally specific, nonascriptive structures (Sutton 1963).

Instead of rewarding ascribed characteristics, such as sex and race, modern societies value achieved characteristics like education and technical skill. This change does not represent enlightenment so much as a practical response to modern life. The moral basis of evaluation of individuals is a reflection of what is important to the survival of the society (Parsons 1940).

Modern industrial society's increasing size and complexity are manifest in a well-developed, highly interdependent occupational system. Property remains a basis of power, but has a new component—skill. Technical skills are developed and owned by individuals to be used in their occupations. These skills constitute a claim on future income, similar to the capitalist's owning of a factory. Neoclassical economists argue that in modern society every worker has become a capitalist because of the importance of labor power to production (Becker 1971).

Income differences among individuals are seen as rational and necessary; because workers must forego earnings to train for difficult occupations, those occupations must be more highly rewarded than occupations requiring little training. The stage of societal development provides the link between the importance of the occupation and the pattern of inequality in the society. As the functional importance of occupations changes, so does the reward structure. Foremost among the available rewards in modern society is income. "Income does not confer prestige on a position so much as it induces people to compete for the position" (Davis and Moore 1945, p. 247). The centrality of income and occupation to the functionalist theory of stratification is apparent in status attainment research, the functionalist theory of age stratification, and human capital research.

Status Attainment Research

The basic problem guiding status attainment research has been the development of a causal model linking occupational mobility to the life cycle of individuals. As a process model, status attainment theory focuses on factors that help explain the transition from occupational origins (father's occupation) to destinations; most of these factors are characteristics of individuals, such as education, intelligence, and ambition. The very definitions of differentiation, inequality, and stratification used by status attainment researchers illustrate the individualistic focus of this research.

The very notion of society entails the concept of *differentiation*. A population is functionally differentiated when some of its members regularly do different things (perform different roles) than others. . . . Institutionalized *inequality* exists when, as a matter of more or less consistent practice, different roles are differently rewarded, when their performance confers status distinctions, or when different performances of a given type of role are differentially evaluated. . . . Social *stratification* refers to the persistence of positions in a hierarchy of inequality, either over the lifetime of a birth cohort of individuals or, more particularly, between generations. (Duncan 1968, pp. 680–81)

The process of social differentiation at the societal level, guided by technical rationality in the division of labor, eventually makes work the most salient characteristic for stratification (Blau and Duncan 1967), and technical skill and individual performance form the basis of allocating people to jobs.

Status attainment researchers have extended the model to include a variety of dimensions of attainment, from occupation to income and net worth.[1] Despite this attention to broader aspects of stratification, the approach is confined by its functionalist theoretical assumptions to focus on individual resources and liabilities, rather than on structural or extraindividual advantages and constraints (see Horan 1978). The underlying concern with individual achievement and mobility implies acceptance of inequality as necessary and inevitable. The restriction of status attainment research to the problem of *stratification* makes this acceptance apparent. "Rank may be highly differentiated, but if there is roughly equal access to unequally ranked position, the society is not highly stratified" (Duncan 1968, p. 696). This idea is perfectly consistent with Parsons's (1940) perception of ranking or "moral evaluation" as a natural tendency of societies and with Davis and Moore's (1945, p. 242) effort to explain "the universal necessity" of stratification and "the roughly uniform distribution of prestige as between the major types of positions in every society."

Status attainment researchers' concern with the status hierarchy of occupations is closely related to the functionalist theory of age stratification, developed by Riley, Johnson, and Foner (1972), which places special emphasis on the extent to which older persons occupy socially important positions. This theory explicitly links historical change (period effects) with the generations involved in it (cohort effects) and the life cycle of individuals (age effects). The influence of functionalist theories of societal change and social stratification are evident in the neglect of the distribution of power within age groups. (See Dowd 1980, pp. 30–34, for a discussion of the contributions and shortcomings of the Riley, Johnson, and Foner model.)

A Functionalist Theory of Age Stratification

Riley, Johnson, and Foner's (1972) formulation of a theory of age stratification has closely followed the tenets of classic functionalism. Applying their model of age stratification to the work force places special emphasis on the process of occupation and reward allocation. Normative age criteria, procedures, and agencies serve to link persons to occupational roles and likewise to transfer persons of particular ages from the work role to the retirement role. Protective devices that hold workers in the work force until retirement time are the same age criteria and allocative devices that mediate their transfer out of the work force. However, safeguards against loss of work do not necessarily guarantee fulfillment of age-graded expectations or rewards for work performance, and failure to maintain these expectations or rewards may contribute ultimately to the decision to retire.

In considering social position in the workplace, Riley, Johnson, and Foner are concerned with the allocation processes of education and training that tend to bestow on younger cohorts the skills in demand in the occupational arenas, reversing the traditional age hierarchy in the work force. Younger workers do not necessarily find themselves in apprentice-type relationships with older workers and may even have positions of authority over older workers. The technological developments of industrialization receive the major portion of credit, or blame, for this reversal of the age hierarchy, since industrialization initially broke the hold of the family-apprentice system. The authors also suggest, however, that further technological developments of automation cannot completely explain the lower position of older workers in factories, since work should be less, rather than more, skilled under conditions of automation.[2] However, some retraining is required with automation to teach workers to be minders rather than manipulators of machines. Employers are less willing to retrain older workers than to retrain younger workers because of the shorter remaining work life of older workers and the belief that they are more difficult to retrain.

Rewards, especially economic ones, are differentially distributed according to the importance and difficulty of positions in the occupational structure. Technical positions are filled on the basis of acquired skills, derived from formal education and training, and the allocation of persons to positions concerned with integration of goals is based on experience. The acquisition of technical skills, those involved with finding the means to a single goal, are fairly highly rewarded to draw talent and motivate training but are subordinate to other positions that concern integration of goals. Income inequality, then, accompanies the bureaucratic organization necessary in large-scale industrial societies. Technical positions will not be as highly rewarded as integrative ones, according to Davis and Moore's (1945) functional theory of stratification, but according to Riley and her coauthors, they will be more readily filled by younger, more highly educated cohorts. Thus younger persons are more likely to be found in technical positions, and older persons in integrative, decision-making positions.

The concentration and scale of industrial society have implications for the proliferation or decline of each of these types of highly rewarded positions. Here modernization theory and other theories of industrial development become important. In general, technological changes enable size of production operations to increase and also facilitate their concentration. While positions requiring higher education and advanced technical skills have allegedly increased with size of production facilities, producing a situation favorable to younger workers, concentration has decreased the number of high-reward positions available to older workers, since decision making becomes concentrated along with production. Cohorts of older workers are, therefore, relatively worse off in terms of industrial society's scarce and desired rewards than are cohorts of younger workers.

   This situation represents a reversal of the traditional age hierarchy that characterized preindustrial societies. Cowgill (1972, p. 11), focusing on political and judicial leadership roles and the elderly, finds "the proportion of the aged who retain leadership roles in modern societies is lower than in pre-industrial societies." This tendency also applies to older workers in economic leadership situations. In industrial societies, knowledge gained from experience loses ground to knowledge gained from technical training because of the pace of social change and rapid obsolescence of once valued skills.

The fact of the matter is that rapid social change, such as the contemporary process of modernization, renders older people obsolete. Their classic role as conservators and transmitters of vital information is destroyed. Much that they know is no longer pertinent, and much that they don't know is essential. (Cowgill 1986, p. 173)

   In postindustrial society, the power base shifts away from property toward technical skill. The character of the stratification system is determined by the division between the scientific and technical classes and those who stand outside. "The rise of the new elites based on skill derives from the simple fact that knowledge and planning . . . have become the basic requisites for all organized action in modern society" (Bell 1976, p. 392). Technical skill becomes an overriding condition of competence for place and position. Political organization is still important, but in all kinds of organization, professionals and technicians are called on to guide decision making. The new proletariat of postindustrial society consists of obsolete workers and the retired who have been rejected and exploited by progress (Touraine 1971).
   In a service society, the most important positions demand new technical skills brought by formal education. There are fears that rapid technological progress will cause workers to become obsolete much sooner in their work lives than is true in industrial societies. The labor intensity of service industries implies that they rely more than manufacturing industries do on labor-embodied technology, "which can usually be upgraded only through a replacement of older workers by new employees" (Singlemann 1978, p. 128). Economic rewards, distributed according to skill and importance in the postindustrial society, place older workers in a disadvantaged position relative to younger workers, in much the same way as they are in industrial societies.
   Closely linked to these theories of development and age stratification are theories of neoclassical economics. This linkage can be illustrated by a brief examination of human capital theory and modernization theory as they have been used to explain the position of older workers. These theories are different elaborations of the same basic assumptions—primary among them, the individual basis of achievement and reward.

Human Capital Theory

In economics, labor is treated as human capital in recognition of the small portion of wages and salaries attributable to raw human labor and the large portion attributable to investment in humans in the form of education and on-the-job training (Becker 1971). Human capital theory emphasizes differences in kind rather than amount of work supplied and describes these differences in terms of the individual's education, ability, experience, and training received on the job. Education and training represent investments that exact a cost from the worker, primarily in the form of earnings foregone. The earnings differences accounted for by human capital variables represent compensations for the cost of obtaining these skills.

In the neoclassical theory of labor markets, the assumption of perfectly competitive markets forms the base; this assumption means that workers and firms each have perfect information, attempt to maximize utilities (in particular earnings), and cannot individually influence the prices given by the market (Kalleberg and Sørensen 1979). Since the labor market resembles a market for other goods, a well-developed price theory can be applied to analysis of labor market phenomena, especially to the earnings-determination process. Wages are seen as jointly determined by supply and demand, though the economic literature has tended to treat demand fluctuations as short-run disturbances, emphasizing instead the stable differences in worker productivity as sources of differences in earnings.

Human capital theory and its macrosociological counterpart, modernization theory, have definite implications for the situation of older workers. In a society where education and training are considered investments that workers make in themselves and where opportunities are concentrated on the young, there will be a cohort effect in earnings inequality. Since modernization, once begun, continues, younger generations will always be displacing older ones in the sector of the labor market comprising the new high-demand, and therefore high-wage, occupations. As experience is accumulated in the modern sectors of the labor market, rewards also accumulate, producing an increase in earnings with age. Earnings rise with age as long as, and only as long as, workers continue to invest in themselves. The incentive to invest declines with age, since one has less time to recoup the income lost during the investment period (Becker 1971). Because older workers are less likely to continue to invest in themselves. their rewards do not continue to increase at the same rate as those of younger cohorts, so that a slight downward curve in earnings for older workers results. Thus, the convex shape of the age-earnings profile predicted by human capital theory coincides with the displacement of older workers in the status hierarchy predicted by modernization theory.

SUMMARY: SOCIETAL CHANGE AND AGE STRATIFICATION

The model of social change I discuss in the first part of this chapter places a great deal of emphasis on technology as a force bringing change, not only to the work world, but also to family and community life. Modernization theory has been used to explain many aspects of social organization, from political decision making to family relations. The system of ranking and rewards is also believed to vary in a predictable way with the society's level of development. Bell's (1976) theory of post-industrial society extends the logic of modernization theory to the emerging postmodern societies.

The theories of stratification I outline in the last part of this chapter explicitly develop the implications of life in modern societies for individuals in various occupational roles. "In the absence of hereditary castes or feudal estates, class differences come to rest primarily on occupational positions and the economic advantages and powers associated with them" (Blau and Duncan 1967, p. vii). Even in the theory of age stratification, occupation is of central importance in explaining the way in which older people are valued. In modern societies they are either excluded from occupational roles (retired) or relegated to occupations with soon-to-be-obsolete skills. Postindustrial society's need for highly trained technical experts is not likely to put older people in favored positions.

Some have argued that since service work is light work compared with the heavy, physical work of manufacturing and extractive industries, women and older workers should have a better chance at equal employment. Similarly, the necessarily close link between production of services and their consumption, attributed to the intangible nature of the product and the difficulty in stockpiling services, offers greater opportunities for part-time employment, which would also aid people, such as women and older persons, who desire employment but are unable to work year-round or full days (Singelmann 1978). However, employment by itself does not confer prestige; the ability of older workers to occupy jobs of importance must also increase. Closing the gap in formal education between age cohorts, a process Palmore and Manton (1974) found associated with higher status of the aged, may help older workers in postindustrial society. The declining value of their experience on the job and the rapidly changing occupational structure, each linked to the pace of technological change, would seem to work against such an optimistic view of age stratification in postindustrial society.

THEORETICAL INTENTIONS AND STRATEGIES

It may seem unusual to trace the theoretical issues surrounding age inequality back to functionalist theories dominant in sociology in the

1950s and 1960s. For several reasons, I have chosen this strategy to lead into a discussion of new structuralism. First, I want to make explicit the assumption of rationality in human behavior underlying functionalist sociology and orthodox economics. Moore (1979, p. 1) defines *modernization* as "rationalization of the ways social life is organized and social activities performed." Rationality suggests that individuals use fact and logic in the choice of instrumental behavior for the achievement of various identified goals. Rationalization suggests that behaviors are organized around causo-analytical, scientific reasoning. Knowledge of cause and effect, rather than experiences of trial and error, guides innovations and human responses to innovation. In the economic world, work is structured according to these principles to achieve efficiency. This rationality extends to the demand for certain types of workers and to the supply of desired traits via investments. In a rational world, incentives influence behavior, market principles guide decision making, and market relations guide interaction. Human capital theorists' view of training and education as investments assumes rationality on the part of workers, just as the structure of rewards given to experience reflects the rationality of employers.

Second, I wish to emphasize the integration of societal change and social stratification in the technical functional perspective. New structuralist theories that separate changes in the societal context from a study of inequality lack the breadth of the functionalist approach. In emphasizing the connection between modernization theory and functionalist theories of stratification (including status attainment, human capital, and age stratification theories), I am pointing to the need for new structuralists to clarify the assumptions of societal change inherent in their theories of stratification.

Finally, though proponents of new structuralism consider functionalism a paradigm in crisis (Colclough and Horan 1983), the individualistic approach of functionalist theories of stratification (whether embodied in age stratification, status attainment, or human capital research) survives in policy and ideology. These explanations still dominate thought about the position of age groups in industrial and postindustrial societies (see final chapter of Cowgill [1986]). To move beyond functionalist interpretations of age in new structuralist research, the theoretical nature of these assumptions must be revealed.

NOTES

1. See Colclough and Horan (1983) for a concise summary of the applications of and alternatives to the status attainment perspective, and Baron and Bielby (1980, pp. 745–46) for a discussion of the industrialism thesis and status attainment research.

3

Transformation: The New Structuralist View

Although we sometimes hear complaints about inconveniences, errors, and dangers brought about by technological changes, such problems are generally considered the price of progress. In functionalist theory, as in everyday life, the terms *change* and *progress* are used virtually interchangeably to describe technology. A different, and generally more skeptical, view of technology is inherent in Marxist social science. Technology is not a neutral force driving society, and technological changes in production are not governed by their own logic. Instead, Marxists view technology as a resource, which classes may use in a variety of ways to further their interests or which they may choose not to use if their interests will be harmed by its introduction (Bonacich 1976). Capitalists generally have the power to develop or resist new technologies, but workers can also get involved; the Luddites in Britain during the Industrial Revolution (see Calhoun 1983) represent one of the most famous examples of worker resistance.

This interpretation of technology as a resource and technological change as the realization of class interests is at odds with the modernization and postindustrial theories of social change discussed in chapter 2. Theories of social inequality implied by Marxist theories of social change are, likewise, different from functionalist theories of stratification. In this chapter, I tie Marxist theories of social change to the stratification literature that has come to be known as new structuralism. Unfortunately, the new structuralist literature is far from theoretically coherent.[1] Rather than focusing on these differences, I emphasize the common theme of power—not individual power, but power residing in groups of social actors and manifest in the employment relation.

After outlining the basic elements of a Marxist theory of social change, I briefly review class, labor market, and economic sector approaches to studying inequality in U.S. capitalism. My goal is not to provide a comprehensive review of all new structuralist research, nor is it to resolve the differences inherent in the position. My goal is to extend the Marxist historiography of social change to the 1980s and to bring Marxist notions of power to bear on the study of earnings differences within the working class. In the final section of this chapter I argue that changes in the U.S. economy will affect the earnings power of various groups of workers, and that age-earnings patterns can serve as indicators of these changes. I am bringing together diverse new structuralist arguments, some of which are clearly not Marxist in their underlying theoretical orientation, to make what is basically a Marxian argument about class interests, class resources, and class struggle.

ORGANIZATIONAL SHIFTS: CAPITALISM DRIVES TECHNOLOGY

Marxist theories of social change are often concerned with transformation of societies from one mode of production to another, such as the change from feudalism to capitalism or from capitalism to socialism.[2] Marxists do not see these changes as functionalists do, that is, as a process occurring gradually, with societal institutions adapting and responding to changes in one another. Instead, changes that bring on new epochs are believed to happen in a revolutionary manner, as a result of conflict and struggle between social classes, not of adaptation to and diffusion of new technologies.

Social actors sharing a common structural position have their class interests defined by their positions in the production system. Class interests are thus embedded in the structure of social relations and are not necessarily consciously held. The conflict between dominant and subordinant social classes reflects the contradictions inherent in the mode of production. In capitalism, contradictions between the institution of private property, which acts as a fetter on change, and the progressive forces of production (labor, technology, and social organization) become manifest in the conflict between the major social classes—the owners of productive property and those who work for them.

This class struggle also brings about changes in the *forms* of production occurring within a particular mode of production. The form of production can be identified by the relations and forces of production at the level of the productive unit. Capitalist societies change in terms of the predominant form of production. For example, competitive capitalism gave way to monopoly capitalism as the relations of capitalists to each other and to their workers modified and were modified by changes in production. Stages of capitalism can be defined by the characteristic patterns of impediments to capital accumulation, not by changes in *what* is produced.

Monopoly capitalism represents a solution to the particular impediments of competitive capitalism; growth in aggregate demand was not keeping pace with the growth of surplus value (Wright 1978). Keynesian policies of state-sponsored waste, the institutionalization of collective bargaining and of complex organizational arrangements within large corporations, and the accomplishment of stability in the international trade and finance system helped resolve these constraints on accumulation.

The solution to the impediment moves capitalism to a new stage but also contains new contradictions that gradually emerge in later stages. Although the capitalist class, by definition, has more power than the working class, working class power can be brought to bear on the accumulation process through labor organization in the workplace (Offe and Wiesenthal 1980) or political influence on the welfare state (Piven and Cloward 1982). The class struggle, therefore, remains central to the process of transformation, even when the transformation is from one form of capitalist production to another rather than from the capitalist mode of production to a socialist one.

An important part of Marxist theories of social change in capitalism is the proletarianization thesis, which holds that the advancement of capitalism will make more people in the society dependent on the sale of their own labor power for subsistence. The petty bourgeoisie (such as the self-employed) diminish in number, and the amount of skill and the discretion of direct producers over their labor are reduced. Within the labor process, proletarianization entails the loss of autonomy and task-oriented decision-making power.

This process is extremely difficult to study quantitatively. Wright and Singelmann (1982), while eschewing occupational categories of the population census, are ultimately forced to rely on them for creating occupation-specific class distributions within industries for 1960 and for 1970.

The authors are forthright in recognizing the "sweeping assumptions" (p. 205) and possible biases (pp. 207–8) involved in their estimation procedure, but they are left with no other feasible way to identify the changes in the class composition within industries and the changes in overall class structure that result from changes in industry structure. Their analysis demonstrates a strong and consistent proletarianization process within industry sectors, though this process is hidden by a countertendency for employment to shift from relatively highly proletarianized industries to those that are relatively less proletarianized, that is, from manufacturing to services.

This analysis of class and the changing structure of capitalism reveals some of the most basic concerns of the critical perspective on societal stratification and change. Even within a democratic capitalist society, power to determine economic returns resides in individuals, not by virtue of their personal characteristics per se, but by virtue of their class membership. Society's most important resources are related to class power.

Power is structural; that is, it is inherent in the position occupied within the organization of production. For example, the structural power of the capitalist comes from ownership of productive property and from control over the means and ends of production. The structural power of workers comes from the embodiment of labor power in them; labor power is the source of surplus value in capitalist production, and surplus value can take the form of profit.

Alternations in the organization of capitalist production will not change this basic relationship between capitalists and workers. However, the ability of one of these social classes to exert its power over the other (and gain relative advantage) does change as capitalism changes. This is because resources available to the class actors are affected by conditions within the work setting, within the economy (at all levels), and within the society. Class struggle is endemic in capitalism because there is a fundamental (structural) conflict between interests of the major social classes, but the results of the class struggle are not predetermined or unchanging.

Burawoy's (1983) analysis of the politics of production focuses on the variable nature of capitalist production relations in Western societies by linking the organization of work to the state. The periodization of capitalism Burawoy develops is not based on the transformation of competition among firms or of the expropriation of skill. Instead, it is based on the transformation in the relationship between workers and wages. State social insurance and protective labor legislation intervened in this relationship by providing a means of livelihood outside of the employment relation and by reducing the dependence of wages on work performance. Under these conditions, "management can no longer rely entirely on the economic whip of the market. . . . Workers must be *persuaded* to cooperate with management" (p. 590, emphasis in original).

According to Burawoy, state intervention in production relations is rooted in the dynamics of capitalism—contradiction and crisis. "But the *mechanisms* through which the state comes to do what is 'necessary' vary over time and from country to country" (p. 591, emphasis in original). And nothing guarantees the success of these interventions. The particular historical circumstances of a society determine the range of options open to the state, but the changes in capitalism at an international level also affect state responses and ultimately production relations in the workplace.

The Marxist views of social change presented above offer different conceptualizations of the stages of capitalism and the role of the state in capitalism. I have stressed their common concern with the structural power of social classes and with the problems posed by the conflict of class interests. These concerns are also present in the stratification literature, in which an important part of the critical perspective has focused on the differential access to resources among workers and the consequences for their economic well-being. These studies are diverse in their formulations but can be grouped according to definitions of structures providing differential opportunities and rewards for workers: class position, labor markets, and economic segments. In the remainder of this chapter, I look briefly at each of these orientations to economic structure, drawing out the implications for social change and stratification according to age.

CLASS THEORIES

Theories of class and income inequality hold that class position shapes the ways in which education and other factors influence income. Class is defined in terms of common structural positions within the social organization of production. In capitalist society, Marxist analysis reveals three criteria underlying the social relations of production: (1) ownership of the means of production, (2) purchase of the labor power of others, and (3) sale of one's own labor power. Traditionally, these criteria have generated three basic class categories: capitalists, workers, and petty bourgeoisie.

Class theorists stress that class categories are not the same as occupational groupings and assert that the class paradigm offers an alternative to the occupational one for understanding inequality.

The term "occupation" designates positions with the *technical* division of labor, i.e., an occupation represents a set of activities fulfilling certain technically defined functions. Class, on the other hand, designates positions within the *social* relations of production, i.e., it designates the social relationship between actors. (Wright and Perrone 1977, p. 35, emphasis in original)

The presence of large corporations in the present era means that the criterion of employing labor power is differentiated between purchasing the labor power of others, done exclusively by capitalists, and controlling the labor power of others, done by capitalists and their managers in the large corporation. Managers emerge as a new social category in corporate capitalism. In the traditional Marxist sense, the petty bourgeoisie are neither workers nor capitalists, but managers have characteristics of both workers and capitalists; since they sell their labor power and control that of others, they are in a "contradictory class location" (Wright 1978).

Results of Wright and Perrone's analysis of income inequality and class position reveal substantial differences between classes in income and in the relationship between education and income. When they control for the effects of variables usually examined in stratification studies (occupational status, age, race, sex, and job tenure), class differences remain. As a variable, class position proves to be at least as powerful as occupational status in explaining income variation. Within class categories, returns to education are similar for blacks and whites and for males and females. The income gap between blacks and whites of the same class is not as great as the one between sexes in the same class, but class differences between managers and workers are considerably greater than the differences between sexes or races within the working class. (A study of wealth in the United States conducted by the Census Bureau in 1984 finds similar differences between self-employed managers and professionals and all groups of employed workers [Kilborn 1986].)

These studies of social class emphasize the importance of class membership in determining economic outcomes of employment. An emphasis on power of capitalists over workers and of some groups over others is common to sociological and radical economic theories of segmented labor markets. This emphasis on positional rather than individual power is common to the variety of formulations of segmented labor market theory. These formulations represent a shift from the primacy of purely economic forces in wage theories to an emphasis on sociological factors (Piore 1973).

LABOR MARKET SEGMENTATION

The basic idea in labor market segmentation is that significant occupational wage differentials are caused by separating workers into non-competing groups (Cain 1976). "To be split, a labor market must contain at least two groups of workers whose price of labor differs for the same work, or would differ if they had the same work" (Bonacich 1972, p. 549). The neoclassical economic models of perfect competition and rationally motivated behavior lost credibility as the economy grew more complex, government regulation of industry became more visible, and anticompetitive institutions, such as labor unions and bureaucratic organizations, proliferated. Thus, theories of labor market segmentation emerged, attempting to explain the persistent inequality in labor market outcomes.

The Process

Reich, Gordon, and Edwards (1973) trace the development of labor market segmentation to the conscious efforts of monopolistic corporations and systematic forces in the development of monopoly capitalism. Attempts of monopoly capitalist corporations to control an increasingly hostile labor force around the turn of the twentieth century involved changes in the internal relations of the firms toward an intensification of hierarchical control. Internal labor markets with well-specified job ladders were structured by firms and cooperative union agreements. Employers used firm-specific benefits to garner lifetime allegiances and consciously exploited race, ethnic, and sex antagonisms to divide and conquer the work force.

Bonacich (1976) disagrees that the black-white split in the labor market was the result of a capitalist plot to gain the loyalty of white workers by paying them more than blacks. She emphasizes instead the historical antecedent of black participation in the U.S. labor force, namely, slavery. Between World War I and the New Deal, the capitalist class was faced with (but did not create) a labor market differentiated in terms of bargaining power. Blacks were more exploitable than most whites, even after the end of slavery, because of the legacy of slavery—extreme poverty and a tradition of paternalism. Racial antagonism among workers was a resource exploited by the capitalist class to undermine strike activity. This perpetuated the circle of white union resistance to membership of blacks and black disinterest in organizing. This circle of racial antagonism among workers was finally broken by New Deal labor legislation, which tended to equalize the price of black and white labor (and, as a result, ultimately to reduce the employment of blacks).

The persistence of peripheral or marginal firms operating on cheap labor means that a split labor market is not dead in this country. Protective legislation has changed its shape somewhat, increasing the segmentation, by industry and plant, of higher priced from cheap labor. . . . But the New Deal did not, in the long run, successfully eradicate the problem. (Bonacich 1976, p. 48)

The growing strength of industrial unions led to a transformation of some firm-specific benefits to industry-wide privileges, helping to foster segmentation by industry. Employers and workers face fundamentally different conditions and operate according to fundamentally different rules in each industrial sector. This development occurred largely as a result of systemic forces in the emergence of the oligopolistic core and in the continued existence of a competitive fringe of industries. The larger, more capital-intensive firms were generally sheltered by barriers to entry. Their advantages came in the areas of technology, market power, and financial economies of scale. This enabled them to generate higher rates of profit and growth than their smaller, labor-intensive competitive counterparts could (Reich, Gordon, and Edwards 1973).

The Consequences

Contemporary theories of segmented labor markets concentrate on the demand characteristics of the role or job occupied. The "complex of rules which determines the movement of workers among job classifications within administrative units, such as enterprises, companies, or hiring halls" constitutes internal labor markets (Dunlop 1966, p. 32). These markets stand in contrast to the external labor market where pricing, allocation, and training decisions are controlled directly by market forces (Kalleberg and Sørensen 1979). However, there is considerable disagreement about the antecedents of and motivations for labor market segmentation. Internal labor markets have been classified as consisting of two major types. The first type is equated with a particular firm; the firm controls entry and workers are promoted along orderly lines of progression. Members of a particular occupational group, usually a craft occupation, control entry and mobility in the second type of internal labor market. A major structural characteristic of internal labor markets is the presence of seniority entitlements.[3]

The debate over the appropriate level of analysis for the study of labor markets has been long and arduous. In their literature review, Althauser and Kalleberg (1981) find internal labor markets variously defined by firms, job ladders, seniority entitlements, and job stability. They offer a new conceptualization of the variety of internal labor markets, occupational labor markets, firm labor markets, and secondary labor markets likely to exist in modern capitalism. These labor markets can be broadly defined as positions in the economy and identified with aggregate data on occupations and industries. Use of an occupation-industry matrix of positions divides workers based on known characteristics of their work rather than on individual characteristics of education, sex, race, or age.

A number of researchers have suggested such an approach to labor markets. (See Kaufman and Spilerman [1982, p. 848] for a discussion of the strengths of an occupation-by-industry analysis to study careers.) Freedman (1976) uses a computer typology construction technique known as Automatic Interaction Detection (AID) to define labor market segments; annual earnings is the criterion on which the segmentation of occupation-industry groups is based. Essentially, her method reverses the logic of labor market theory; similar earnings groups are discovered via the structural (demand-side) or demographic (supply-side) characteristics that account for earnings variation. She thus groups together positions with similar characteristics and refers to these groups as labor markets. This atheoretical approach to labor market segmentation does little to reveal the dynamics operating in the labor market. It runs counter to the definition of labor markets as arrangements offering differential rewards (of which income is one) to those with similar skills or educational attainment.

Although not couched theoretically, Freedman's study provides evidence consistent with one theory of social change and labor markets: the polarization of workers and positions into privileged and vulnerable groups. The power of worker groups at the top of the earnings structure is secured by changes generating positions for professionals. However, more and more workers are in vulnerable positions. Freedman's analysis reveals a loss of middle-earnings positions between 1960 and 1970.

Young workers and females were the big losers; their overrepresentation in the bottom earnings segments increased from 1960 to 1970. When earnings segments were defined by demographic characteristics, the most influential variable in 1960, age, became even more important in 1970; sex declined somewhat in its contribution to explained variance; race dropped out completely. Freedman emphasizes that the change in the influence of race may be deceptive since only the employed are included in the analysis.

A final point from the Freedman study: she found no relationship between employment growth or decline and changes in earnings.

In particular, earnings increases do not result directly from employment growth. Given the right conditions, earnings may show relative as well as absolute increases in sectors where employment is declining relatively, or even absolutely. A long period of depressed demand may slow down the rate of wage increases, but in this case also, worker groups with bargaining power can maintain their *relative* positions in the earnings structure vis-à-vis unsheltered worker groups. (1976, p. 17, emphasis in original)

Whereas dual labor market writers tend to focus on such characteristics as "wages, working conditions, chances for advancement, and employment stability as delimiters of sectoral distinctions," researchers in the dual economy tradition focus on industrial structure and the economic organization of production as the basis of sectoral distinctions and view labor market segmentation as a *consequence* of segmentation in the economic order (Tolbert, Horan, and Beck 1980, p. 1096). Both sectoral perspectives find earnings, unemployment, and compositional differences existing among the various sectors, and both argue that structural features of the economy mediate the process by which individual characteristics are rewarded. Thus, sectoral differences have important implications for the opportunity structures and experiences that individual workers face. Before discussing the research dealing with stratification and economic segmentation, I briefly review a key work that has provided the foundation for industry and firm models of segmentation.

THE DUAL ECONOMY

In his seminal work on the dual economy, Averitt (1968) defines the business organization of the U.S. industrial system as consisting of a center economy and a periphery economy. The pure conglomerate represents the ultimate center firm in that it is not built around a specific market and is highly decentralized, leaving initiative well below the level of top management. Firms in the periphery are grouped according to their relationship with the economic center into (1) satellites whose output is derived from demand for the center firm's product but that are totally isolated from the center firm's market, (2) the loyal opposition that comprises the competitive fringe, and (3) the residual category of free agents, most of whom operate on the economic fringes of the raw material-manufacturing-retail continuum.

Center firms have many advantages in the dual economy: their extensive assets allow them to spend more, and lose more, than peripheral industries; they maintain better geographic and product diversification, enabling them to withstand losses in one area indefinitely; they can become their own supplier and distributor; the loyal opposition provides a buffer against the full impact of market downturn, since consumers tend to stick with national brands; and they have advantages in obtaining credit, access to mass media, and political and legal situations. At least some of the advantages come from the existence of the periphery as an arena where risk is absorbed. The center's continued existence, then, depends in part on continued existence of the periphery.

Business dualism also has implications for labor economics. Labor unions tend to be found in the center-controlled key industries because of certain market characteristics of these industries. In key industries, sales are more dependent on aggregate demand then on small price variations. As a result, center firms are able to pass wage increases on to their customers through higher prices when aggregate demand is climbing but need not lower prices when aggregate demand falters. In addition, because of the center's monopoly-pricing power, union demands for higher wages can be met without cutting into profits. The large firm size in the center also contributes to union strength; workers, being more distant for management in large firms, are more willing to join a union than are those in smaller periphery firms. Because of similarities in the production process of the center firms (large batch or continuous flow), labor costs represent a relatively small portion of total costs.

Unions also aid the center economy, first by setting uniform standards for wage rates that tend to extend to present and potential center firm competitors, presenting an additional barrier to their entry into the center. Second, wage rates are known for the life of the contract, preventing unplanned wage increases during periods of labor scarcity and thereby facilitating long-range planning. Unions also provide security from unauthorized labor unrest and insurance against government intervention in wages and labor conditions. However, unions do face certain impediments to labor objectives in center industries. These impediments stem from the existence of the loyal opposition and backward satellites in the periphery and from realities of an international economy, which presents the constant threat of migration of center firms to other nations.

Averitt concentrates on transformative industries, pointing to the heavy reliance of a developed economy on manufacturing for its income and employment and to the supportive role social capital industries (intermediate producer industries—transportation, communication, and public utilities) play in manufacturing. However, his analysis of the dual economy has been extended to include service industries as well.

Industry Models of the Dual Economy

Sociologists eager to study the effects of economic segmentation have refined the distinction between sectors of the dual economy, but their classification schema keeps within the general distinction of oligopoly and competitive capitalism suggested by Averitt and other leaders in the dual economy tradition (see Bluestone, Murphy, and Stevenson 1973; Edwards 1975; Gordon 1972). For example, the empirical indicators of market structure that Tolbert, Horan, and Beck (1980) use fall into three basic categories: (1) measures of the capacity for oligopoly in an industry, most centrally market concentration but also economic scale; (2) measures of oligopolistic behavior in the industrial product market (profit levels, advertising expenditures, and political contributions); and (3) measures of oligopolistic behavior in the industrial labor market (extent of internal labor market development and relative size of the bureaucratic work force).

In an earlier study, Beck, Horan, and Tolbert (1978) attributed approximately one-third of the sectoral discrepancy in workers' earnings ($3,057.97 per average worker in 1975) to differences between the core and periphery in rates of return on worker characteristics. The other two-thirds reflected differences in labor force quality. They also found that being female or nonwhite has significant negative effects on annual earnings in the core, effects not apparent in the periphery, suggesting that discrimination within the core works to the advantage of white males. Discrimination seems to play a part in channeling female and nonwhite workers into the periphery; females constitute 54 percent of the periphery, compared with 29 percent of the core, and nonwhites represent 11 percent of the periphery and 9 percent of the core (Tolberg, Horan, and Beck 1980).

Although there have been some treatments of the development of the dual economy and the advancement of monopoly capitalism, there has been little examination of changes in the outcomes to workers across time in advanced capitalism. The important forces at work in the transformation of society are those increasing the power of corporate actors: increased concentration and centralization. These increases would be apparent in growth of the monopoly sector and would enable these employers to provide even higher wages to their workers, increasing the income inequality between core and periphery workers. Hodson (1978) examines this hypothesis and finds the ratio of inequality of income of workers in monopoly and competitive sectors stable over a 30-year period.

Featherman and Hauser (1978) consider the net effects of employment in industrial segments (an extension of Hodson's classification) on earnings in 1962 and 1973. Although the purpose of their analysis is to compare it with their status attainment model, the sectoral comparisons over time are unique and give a sense of the direction of change. Their analysis shows an increase in the degree of inequality within each segment and a reduction in the ability of structural features to explain men's earnings. These findings are consistent with Freedman's (1976); she finds that industrial concentration was not an important variable for defining earnings sectors in 1970, though it had been in 1960. Featherman and Hauser conclude that their data "suggest a declining significance of 'structural' features of the economy for the acquisition of relative earnings" (1978, p. 492).

Company-Level Segmentation and the Organization of Work

Among early critics of the dual economy position, Baron and Bielby (1980) distinguished themselves from those whose critiques were primarily empirical or methodological in nature (cf. Zucker and Rosenstein 1981) by arguing that organizational arrangements within firms provide the explanatory link between macrolevel processes of societal differentiation and microlevel dimensions of inequality and position. They contend that disagreements among the new structuralist perspectives largely reflect different views of what is going on within firms, specifically about the motivations of decision makers. It is the organizational arrangements within firms that are important, but these arrangements are obscured by industry-level analysis.

Taking the criticisms of industry-level segmentation into account, Hodson (1983, 1984) develops a model of segmentation among firms. His company-level model does not specifically address the concerns voiced by Baron and Bielby, especially the discovery of the motivations of decision makers, but does move closer to an organizational analysis than do other sectoral models. In comparing the strength of industry-level and company-level models of labor force earnings, he finds that employee earnings are more directly influenced by work organization than by product market organization. The company-level model that best explains earnings of both men and women is composed of three sectors: monopoly (large, nationally prominent companies), multiplant (companies with plants outside the immediate local area), and local (companies based entirely in one area). The single most important variable is plant employment size. Overall, organizational and technical dimensions of size and capital use are more important for wage determination than the market factors associated with firms or industries.

Employee earnings do not appear to be tied to the level of company profits, and higher wages do not appear to be the result of management strategies to create a stable and compliant labor force where this is allowed by monopoly profits. Rather, we would argue that wage increases are won by employees in certain sectors based partially on the resources provided by the organization of the workplace. (Hodson 1983, p. 196)

Hodson emphasizes that his theoretical argument is not a corollary of Bell's (1976) thesis "that in postindustrial society greater education and skill requirements of production produce heightened equality and order in society. Rather, the argument is that the organizational structure of modern enterprises potentially empowers workers to seek the attainment of improved conditions" (Hodson 1983, p. 197). Regarding the direction of the development of industrial structure and its impact on the workplace, Hodson briefly notes that new forms of workplace organization have broad implications for social stratification. These changes include post–World War II increases in average firm size and national-level concentration, growth of conglomerates, and rise of multinational corporations.

Despite these references to new forms of organization, new structuralists have failed overall to address the changing conditions of worker power within economic sectors. In chapter 4, I discuss the changes in the nature of late U.S. capitalism. In doing so, I hope to strengthen the new structuralist perspective by sharpening its focus on power and class resources. In preparation for that discussion, I next offer a new structuralist interpretation of the age-earnings relationship.

AGE AND THE NEW STRUCTURALIST CRITIQUE

Although criticisms of the new structuralist model's theoretical development exist (Hodson and Kaufman 1982; Kalleberg, Wallace, and Althauser 1981; Zucker and Rosenstein 1981), sociologists seeking to improve the status attainment model of inequality generally agree that new structuralists have properly focused attention on the context in which individual behavior occurs. The neoclassical model of inequality reviewed in chapter 2 (human capital theory in economics and functionalist theory of stratification in sociology) emphasizes individual rationality and characteristics of labor supply as primary determinants of earnings. Earnings differences between men and women, whites and nonwhites, young and old can be explained by differences in education, ability, experience, training, and labor market commitment (Becker 1971). New structuralists emphasize that the economy is divided along structural lines into distinct sectors providing different opportunities and rewards for individual characteristics. These sectors reflect the differences in power among capitalists and among workers.

Marxist economists Samuel Bowles and Herbert Gintis's (1975) critique of human capital theory illustrates the new structuralist preoccupation with power. They argue that human capital theorists' treatment of the labor-wage exchange as a pure market exchange excludes consideration of the power of capitalist over worker. Ownership and control structures of the firm determine not only the incentive and control mechanisms over workers but also the types of workers' coalitions possible. Ascriptive characteristics of race, sex, and age are used to fragment the work force, thereby reducing potential coalitions.

Interpretations of Worker Characteristics

Bowles and Gintis (1975) take issue with human capital theorists' quantitative interpretation of background characteristics. Families and schools teach different things to different people, not simply more or less (see also Bowles and Gintis 1976). Bowles and Gintis do not deny that capitalists offer an economic return to schooling and age; however, they see this as part of the capitalists' need to legitimate and reproduce the power structure of the firm.

Black and female workers, who are by and large excluded from exercising authority over any but workers of their own sex and race, are likely for this reason to earn lower returns to schooling. Moreover, less well educated workers are, for the same reason, unlikely to gain a high rate of return to aging. (Bowles and Gintis 1975, p. 80)

Implicit in the new structuralist critique of neoclassical economic theory is this assumption that human capital variables have other meanings. Education reflects not just some sort of training, but a credential, a screening device (Collins 1979; Freedman 1976). Gender is a proxy for human capital because being female signals intermittent labor force participation, a lack of commitment. But structuralists argue that skills are undervalued in typically female occupations (the basis of comparable worth lawsuits) and that female gender serves as a signal for cheap, exploitable labor. "Analysts in the structuralist tradition interpret the existence of sex and race differences in earnings as indicative of systematic forces involving differential opportunity structures which are embedded in the socioeconomic order" (Beck, Horan, and Tolbert 1978, pp. 708–9).

Age, too, has several meanings in the earnings determination process. Human capital theorists see age as a proxy for experience. But, as years of experience are accumulated in one's job, they are also accumulated on one's body. Aging, therefore, represents both accumulation of experience and physical decline in strength and stamina. For a time, the value of experience offsets physical changes. Earnings rise with age as long as the investment in a worker's skills continues and performance is not hampered by physical decline. Most workers reach a point, however, where the incentive for further investment, by themselves and by their employers, is low. After middle age, little work life remains to recoup costs of retraining or updating skills. This disincentive, combined with physical changes, offsets the value of accumulated experience, bringing wages down for older workers relative to younger ones. Cross-sectional analysis of the labor force reveals a convex shape in age-earnings profiles (Becker 1971; Stolzenberg 1975). Clark, Kreps, and Spengler (1978) note that the higher the level of education or skill, the later the age at which income is maximized.

However, age also can be seen in a way that functionalists and new structuralists have neglected—as a correlate of worker power. Where workers have institutionalized their power through seniority provisions in collective bargaining agreements or where employers have established internal job ladders to hold valuable (market-powerful) workers, older workers' earnings remain at least as high as those of middle-aged workers. The age-earnings profiles, rather than being convex, have a high plateau shape or even a continued upward slope.

Examples

There are several good examples of this structuralist interpretation of age and earnings. Stolzenberg's (1975) analysis of within-occupation differences in wage attainment is based on an argument that labor markets are segmented along occupational lines. Labor supply and demand play a role in this fragmentation, but so do "social factors such as judgments about the worth of work and patterns of social organization among workers and employers" (p. 646). Looking at similar types of occupations, Stolzenberg finds that age-earnings profiles of workers in more heavily unionized occupations decline less after they peak than do profiles of workers in less unionized occupations.

Even though Stolzenberg's argument about the occupational fragmentation of industries has more in common with the literature on dual labor markets than it does with the dual economy literature, he makes several points about unionization and wage setting that are relevant to the differences among industries; these also are found in Averitt's work on the dual economy (1968). First, unionization changes the wage-setting process from negotiations between individuals to negotiations between formal organizations. Second, the normative economic ideal of perfect competition in the labor market is violated by the monopolistic role of unions (a single seller) and the monopsonistic role of employers (a single buyer). Finally, Stolzenberg notes that unions traditionally emphasize job security and economic protection for their middle-aged and their older members. We see this today in the union contracts that sacrifice wages of future employees (the unborn) for guaranteed benefits for present employees and that create a two-tiered wage structure (Harris 1983). Averitt (1968) notes that these characteristics of pattern bargaining typify center-controlled key industries and offer advantages, such as industry-wide wage structures, to center firms.

Bluestone and others (1981) use age-earnings profiles of retail workers to reveal changes in retail-industry social organization. They find the trend toward corporate hierarchical structure between 1957 and 1975 apparent in the changed shape of white men's age-earnings profiles. Prior to 1972, the profiles were relatively flat for groups over age twenty-five; the highest incomes went to men fifty-five and older. The 1972 and 1975 age-earnings profiles were much steeper and more peaked, with the highest incomes going to men between thirty-five and fifty-four, the corporate managers. White women's age-earnings profiles also changed during this period, but in the opposite way; they became flatter. Bluestone and his coauthors see this flattening as a reflection of the trend away from full-time, commissioned sales positions toward part-time, deskilled cashier positions.

The crucial factor in the Bluestone study of the retail industry is not the social organization of workers (unionization), but the social organization of employers. Ownership has become more centralized, but the pricing remains very competitive. Large department stores continue to invest in new technology that helps deskill jobs, but unions cannot offer promises of substantial wage or benefit increases. The result is union and non-union wage and benefit packages that are almost identical and a retail industry that provides only marginal employment opportunities for most of its work force.

I believe these studies show that age-earnings patterns are useful objects of study. The age-earnings relationship can reveal changes in the social organization of workers and employers, changes that are often obscured by average earnings figures. This is true because age is more than a proxy for experience or an indicator of physical strength and endurance. It is also a correlate of worker power. This is not to say that age confers power. Rather, when privileges accompany age, it is because of power held by the group of workers in general, not just by older workers.

The power workers hold within economic sectors is the subject of chapter 4. The changes that have occurred in the postwar U.S. economy will have had their most profound effect on the power of core-sector workers to secure a high rate of return on their human capital characteristics. The core sector is the most interesting theoretically because its workers, having attained more influence over the earnings process than workers in the periphery, have more to lose. I am not suggesting that periphery workers will be immune from economic changes. Their earnings are affected by national and international competition, as well as by the institutionalized power of the working class (minimum wage levels).

NOTES

1. For critical overviews of new structuralist research see Baron and Bielby (1980) and Hodson and Kaufman (1982).

2. The mode of production has its own laws of motion, existing at two distinct but mutually dependent levels: the productive unit and the economy. Capitalism is a mode of production characterized by wage relations at the enterprise level and by competition and markets at the economy level. Social change of the broad epochal variety is the transformation of a society from one mode of production to another, brought about by contradictions inherent within each (Friedmann 1981).

3. This situation tends to complicate the classificatory scheme somewhat, since it limits the utility of using the age-earnings curve in identifying labor markets. Typically, a positive relationship between age and earnings exists in internal labor markets and a flat curve characterizes this relationship in the external labor market. However, as Spilerman (1977, p. 583) argues, "if we identify an internal labor market with a situation in which seniority entitlements bind a firm to its workers and workers to the firm, internal labor markets will exist even where the potential for earnings growth and promotion is no better than it is in the secondary sector."

4

Age, Earnings, and Change within Economic Sectors

Older workers are powerful to the extent that the organizations to which they belong are powerful. Some older workers belong only to the work organization and deal with it as individuals. Others are members of organizations that represent them in the work setting. In the first case, rewards to the individual are allocated according to principles of competition in the market for labor. But earnings are not influenced only by individual characteristics; new structuralists argue that economic or industrial structure has consequences for the outcomes of labor force participation. Economic structure has been shown to influence workers' earnings whether or not they are represented by second-order organizations, most commonly labor unions, within the workplace (Hodson 1983).

From this perspective, the stratification of age groups reflects the structural constraints of the economy in which workers of various ages participate. This is contrary to the functionalist argument that age stratification is the result of the allocation of people to socially valued roles (Riley, Johnson, and Foner 1972), a process dependent on training and educating individuals for the important and difficult occupations and guided by technological developments that make older workers obsolete (Cowgill 1972; Touraine 1971). However, I believe there has been a change in the reward structure for workers. Because age has been a correlate of workers' power in the core sector of the economy, changes in the distribution of economic rewards to age groups can be used as evidence of changes in the power of workers and employers within sectors of the U.S. economy.

Transformation in U.S. advanced capitalism has occurred in what is produced and in how production is organized. The monopolistic and competitive forms of production, characteristic of the capitalist mode of production in the twentieth century, are undergoing changes that will affect economic outcomes for workers. Concentration of capital and market power, which provided the basis for analysis of industrial segmentation into oligopolistic and competitive categories, remains an important element in understanding advanced capitalism. Indeed, the suggestions of greater concentration in the U.S. economy in the 1980s seem only to be stating the obvious, and to some the inevitable, in light of the recent wave of merger activity. However, new structuralist formulations have generally failed to address the changing conditions of class power within economic sectors.

The various positions I have grouped together in the previous chapter under the umbrella term *new structuralism* in one way or another define the structure of social relations in production as important to the stratification of workers. In each position, there is evidence of a tension abiding within the social structure between classes, labor markets, or economic sectors. Common to all is a critique (sometimes implicit) of individualistic theories of stratification and technological theories of social change. However, problems to be addressed and potentials to be developed remain. Below, I briefly outline some of these problems and potentials.

PROBLEMS AND POTENTIALS IN THE NEW STRUCTURALISM

The most basic criticism of the new structuralism has been directed at its descriptive character. Hodson and Kaufman (1982) charge that development of the theory has been constrained by the assumption that dual labor market structure is parallel to dual economic structure—good jobs in the core, dead-end jobs in the periphery. This parallelism has made it "impossible to investigate the relationship between economic and labor market structure and to evaluate their potentially distinct impacts on working conditions" (p. 735). In their empirical examination of the various models of economic segmentation, Zucker and Rosenstein (1981) conclude that there is a clear need for further development of the underlying theoretical model of new structuralism.

The emphasis on quantitative measures of structure and outcomes has distracted researchers from understanding the dynamic process implied by the term *segmentation* (see Wilkinson 1981). Process is inferred by changes in outcomes (Wright and Singelmann 1982); structures are stagnant entities defined by ratios, size, and scale. The model-testing approach directs attention to the amount of variance explained and away from the ability to comprehend the resulting models. Freedman's (1976) analysis generated 14 labor market segments from 1970 data, 16 from 1960 data. In addition to continuous-variable models for companies and industries, Hodson (1983) gives us a three-sector company-level and a six-sector industry-level model (down from 16 sectors derived from typology construction techniques). Understanding the structural impediments and constraints on class actions and motives and the relationships of the structures to each other is complicated by so many categories.

This is not to say that power can only be understood by dividing the world into two camps—the strong and the weak, the good guys and the bad guys, the exploiters and the exploited. However, for all its empirical weaknesses and its conspiratorial theories of capitalist plots, the dualist historiography succeeds in giving us a sense of the relationship of sectors to each other by capturing the essence of struggle, contradiction, even as it fails to note its ongoing nature. However, dualists are guilty of overemphasizing the power of the capitalist class and of neglecting the structures that empower workers (Hodson 1983; Hodson and Kaufman 1982; Kalleberg, Wallace, and Althauser 1981). To the extent that new structuralist thought has focused on economic segments as static structures leading to set outcomes for workers, it is deterministic in nature. Like technological determinists, economic determinists fail to take into account the interactional nature of class relationships and the effect of the class struggle on historical transformations. Historical variability in the resources stemming from the organization of production is not considered (Hodson and Kaufman 1982) and the resources stemming from the politics of production are generally neglected (Burawoy 1983).

A Resource Perspective

Hodson and Kaufman (1982) suggest a "resource perspective" to supplement contributions of the dual approach. This perspective emphasizes the interactional nature of power relationships. Dualists have stressed the creation and manipulation of economic structure by the capitalist class, to the neglect of labor's role and of the resources and vulnerabilities such structures pose for labor. Hodson and Kaufman examine several dimensions of economic sectors using a resource approach and suggest possible outcomes for workers and capitalists. Several of the power resources they examine are especially pertinent to a discussion of transformations in the postwar economy.

Large firm size has represented a structural resource to workers and owners. "Large firms have the resources to manipulate the environment in which they operate in order to maximize profits. . . . From the standpoint of labor, workers in large firms have greater possibilities for communication and organization than workers dispersed in a multitude of small shops" (Hodson and Kaufman 1982, p. 736). The large size of the mass-production industrial facility is used as an example of the way in which size serves as a resource for workers.

Conglomerate organization provides increased efficiency for capital through improved internal coordination. This form of organization is also advantageous for labor, because it offers the possibility of gaining union toeholds in new industries by following the parent company into new production activities. In contrast, the multinational corporate form—the model core firm according to Averitt (1968)—offers many advantages to capital but comparatively few to labor.

These examples of class resources put economic structure in a more dynamic, less deterministic light. However, Hodson and Kaufman fail to consider completely the implications of larger economic changes on the ability of workers to use organizational forms as class resources. They continue the new structuralist preoccupation with manufacturing industries and neglect of service industries. For example, in their discussion of large firm size as a resource for workers, they fail to differentiate between company size and establishment size. Communication and organizational resources for workers come with establishment size, not firm size. Although the two existed together in manufacturing industries, service industries are less likely to have a large establishment accompanying a large company. In this situation, workers' power in the core sector of the economy may be decreasing over time, particularly if service industries come to gain greater representation in the core than has been true in the past.

They also argue that the conglomerate organizational form represents a significant possibility for service industry workers, but they fail to consider that successful unionization in services will be conditioned by a variety of other circumstances, including larger societal attitudes surrounding unionization. Their example of the Teamsters' successful organization of loading dock and lower white-collar workers with whom they have come into contact does not appear to provide a realistic assessment of the potential that conglomerate organization offers to workers who have little contact with workers from the heavily unionized industries of durable manufacturing and distributive services. It is difficult to see conglomerate organization as a resource for workers in the producer services of finance and real estate.

The conclusions Hodson and Kaufman reach about labor's disadvantage in the multinational corporate form have wide support (see Babson 1973; Barnet and Müller 1974; Bluestone and Harrison 1982). Labor is vulnerable to threats of lost jobs to the global labor market if it does not accept the offerings of capital. This vulnerability may reduce the advantages core workers had gained in the era prior to dominance of the multinational firm. But the overseas threat is not confined to workers in multinational companies. Vulnerabilities come from the global product market and affect workers in entire industries. Thus, workers across the unionized durable manufacturing industries of the core find the gap narrowing between their wages and those in the service industries of the periphery.

Service Economy: Complications

The development of a service economy within advanced capitalism should complicate the debates about the organization of production, but this has not happened. In her paper on "missed opportunities and neglected directions," Sullivan (1981, p. 335) notes a few problems for labor market conceptualization of the development of the service sector: "Service workers in self-owned or very small enterprises simultaneously sell their labor (in the labor market) and their service (in the commodity market). The services rendered and the characteristics of the workers cannot be distinguished."

Conceptualization of the economy as capital markets has also missed the implications of the growth of services. Indeed, one of the key works within this tradition is an analysis of the organization of manufacturing industries (Averitt 1968). Although those who have struggled to provide an empirically derived model of economic segmentation have included all industry types, from agriculture and mining to personal services (Hodson 1978; Tolbert, Horan, and Beck 1980), the relevance for services of the criteria used has not been made explicit.

Granovetter (1984, p. 331) points out one of the problems of this neglect: "While average weekly wages of employees in manufacturing rise almost monotonically with establishment size—as suggested by dual-economy arguments—there is almost no correlation between these wages and establishment size in services." He further contends that it is unclear that "the kinds of arguments adduced to explain the peripheral status of small manufacturing firms can readily be generalized beyond manufacturing." The declining proportion of private-sector workers involved in manufacturing industries, now one in four, suggests the importance of addressing the role of services in the dual economy.

Stanback and Noyelle (1982) insist that the ushering in of the service economy has entailed change in both what is produced and in how production is organized. In terms of the what of production, major shifts in employment since World War II can be traced to the increased role of government and nonprofit and producer services and to the declining importance of agriculture and manufacturing. The organization of production has changed in service and nonservice industries alike, in part because of the increased size of the market and the rise of large corporations. The result has been a greater polarization between skilled and unskilled workers and a growing dichotomy based on pay and mobility between good and bad jobs even in oligopolistic firms. "At a theoretical level," according to Stanback and Noyelle (1982, p. 142), "this simply says that a new kind of segmentation has become more important and that the conventional interpretation is becoming more and more out of step with empirical reality."

To investigate the validity of this change, social scientists must analyze how changes in the organization of production and in what is produced have affected the power of workers to obtain favorable outcomes in their earnings. The organization of production extends beyond the firm and is subject to change. The potentials of new structuralist research lie in widening the resource perspective to examine how changes in the what and the how of production have affected the resources available to workers and owners within economic sectors. In this chapter, I examine changes in U.S. industrial structure in the post–World War II period and draw out implications for workers' earnings and inequality of age groups.

CHANGE IN THE DUAL ECONOMY: GLOOMY EXPECTATIONS

In 1968 Averitt characterized the center economy as primarily manufacturing firms of large economic size, vertically integrated, geographically dispersed, and managerially decentralized. With abundant financial resources, large cash flows, and excellent credit opportunities, center firms were able to buy labor peace while increasing their share of the market; they were able to spend more and lose more than their competition. Geographic and product diversification enabled them to withstand losses in one area indefinitely. Unions aided the center economy, according to Averitt, by providing uniformity of wage rates across the industry, a barrier to center economy entry by competitors. Through the labor contract, center planning was facilitated; wage rates were known for the life of the contract, preventing unplanned wage increases during periods of labor scarcity.

This picture of the center economy was central to the sociological work that drew parallels among earnings inequality, labor market structure, and industrial organization. However, changes in labor's position in the dual economy were also hypothesized in this early work. Averitt saw a dim future for center labor, suggesting that high wages would increase the propensity of center management to substitute physical and human capital for labor. He saw a hostile environment for future union growth, pointing out that the easily organized manufacturing firms had unions, leaving nonunionized the geographically dispersed plants of relatively small size. Increases in white-collar employment, participation of women in the labor force, and employment in the South presented major obstacles to union growth. Trends in labor force participation and industrial growth since Averitt wrote *The Dual Economy* have been consistent with these gloomy expectations for center labor.

Occupational and industrial shifts, combined with economic decline in the 1970s, produced an increase in the proportion of the labor force in white-collar occupations. Census data illustrate the extent of this shift (see table 4.1). Professional, technical, and managerial occupations increased from 17.7 percent of the labor force in 1960 to 26.4 percent in 1980. Employment in the transformative industries dropped from 40.1 percent in 1960 to 31.7 percent in 1980. Women increased their share of total employment in the civilian (nonextractive) labor force from 39 to 47 percent between 1960 and 1980. In addition to these changes in labor force composition, changes have occurred in the employment setting. Work is done increasingly in smaller-sized establishments (Granovetter 1984), in nonmetropolitan settings (Summers et al. 1976), and in the South and West (Bluestone and Harrison 1982). Despite large numbers of jobs lost through plant closings and contractions, the Sun Belt experienced a net gain of 4 percent in its share of private-sector jobs between 1969 and 1976 (Bluestone and Harrison 1982, p. 30).

The decline in union representation is apparent not only in the proportion of all workers who belong to unions (down from 35 percent in 1954 to 24 percent in 1978), but also in the share of plant workers with collective bargaining agreements. In 1960, 73 percent of plant workers were protected by these agreements; in the 1974 to 1976 period, only 61 percent were protected (U.S. Department of Labor 1980). This shift may be especially significant for older workers; the earnings of older union members average 19 percent higher than those of their nonunion counterparts (Freeman and Medoff 1984). Furthermore, since expanding industries tend to employ young workers (Kaufman and Spilerman 1982), the decline of goods-producing industries is shown in a higher average age for workers. Wernick and McIntire (1980) found that by 1978 the proportion of workers under age 35 in manufacturing fell below the average for all industries, although it had been above the average in 1968. Older workers are concentrated in declining industries at a time when union protection in these industries is less extensive.

**Table 4.1 Labor Force Distribution by Capital Sectors,
(in percentages) 1960 and 1980**

Characteristic	All Sectors		Periphery		Core	
	1960	1980	1960	1980	1960	1980
Age						
≤24	19.5	25.8	23.4	30.3	15.9	20.9
25–34	21.8	27.4	19.6	25.5	23.7	29.5
35–44	23.1	18.1	20.8	16.7	25.2	19.6
45–54	19.0	14.7	18.5	13.3	19.5	16.2
55–64	12.2	10.8	12.4	10.3	12.1	11.3
65+	4.4	3.2	5.3	3.9	3.6	2.4
Occupation						
Professional	11.9	14.8	15.1	18.9	8.8	10.5
Manager	5.8	11.6	5.7	10.7	6.0	12.5
Clerical	18.0	17.5	13.3	13.4	22.3	21.9
Sales	8.2	8.7	12.7	13.2	4.1	3.9
Crafts	14.3	12.0	6.9	6.9	21.2	17.6
Operatives	21.9	15.1	17.0	9.0	26.3	21.6
Service	13.9	14.3	24.7	22.7	4.1	5.2
Laborers	6.0	6.0	4.6	5.2	7.3	6.8
Years of Education						
None	0.7	0.3	0.8	0.3	0.5	0.2
1–7	10.7	3.3	11.3	3.5	10.8	3.2
8	13.6	3.4	13.2	3.3	14.0	3.5
9–11	22.3	14.0	23.2	15.2	21.4	12.7
12	30.1	37.9	27.2	34.7	32.8	41.3
13–15	12.5	22.3	12.4	21.9	12.5	22.6
16	5.9	10.0	6.4	10.1	5.4	9.8
17+	4.0	8.9	5.6	10.9	2.5	6.7
Race						
White	89.5	85.2	86.2	84.4	92.5	86.0
Nonwhite	10.5	14.8	13.8	15.6	7.5	14.0
Sex						
Male	61.2	53.2	46.8	41.8	74.2	65.6
Female	38.8	46.8	53.2	58.2	25.8	34.4
Industry						
Transformative	40.1	31.7	13.6	9.7	64.6	50.3
Service	59.9	68.3	86.4	90.3	35.4	49.7
Total	100.0	100.0	47.7	52.0	52.3	48.0

Source: U. S. Bureau of the Census, public use files (one-in-one thousand sample) of the *Censuses of Population and Housing, 1960* and of the *Census of Population and Housing, 1980* (A sample).

Note: See Chapter 5 for description of data and sectors.

Other changes that will affect the power of labor are also occurring within the postwar center economy. These transformations are slightly more obtuse because they involve the organization of core production. Of these, changes in concentration and centralization of capital are of primary importance. Sociologists in the new structuralist tradition have tended to assume that concentration and centralization are increasing in advanced capitalism (see Hodson 1978), but economists tend not to agree with this assumption (see Shepherd 1982).

CLASS RESOURCES AND THE ORGANIZATION OF PRODUCTION

Centralization, Concentration, and Competition

Centralization of capital, the process by which existing capital is redistributed into fewer hands, is reflected by the number of firms within an industry and in the society. Mergers of firms producing essentially the same product are referred to as horizontal mergers. By contrast, vertical mergers involve the joining of firms that represent various stages in the entire production process and conglomerate mergers involve the joining of firms with totally different products or services. Horizontal merger activity has declined in importance since 1926, when it represented 75 percent of merger activity. In modern times, conglomerate activity has come to represent over 80 percent of all corporate mergers (Bluestone and Harrison 1982, p.124). Prominent periods of merger activity since World War II have been those occurring from 1949 to 1955, from 1964 to 1968, and from 1973 to the present. Merger activity yields fewer and more powerful organizations and is closely related to the growing concentration of economic power.

Concentration usually refers to the proportion of sales in a particular industry controlled by a small number of companies. Measures of the proportion of total industry sales attributable to the four largest firms in each industry are known as concentration ratios. In table 4.2 these ratios show the increase in industrial concentration in the United States from 1947 through 1972. However, four-firm concentration ratios ignore imports, which have increased in many U.S. markets. Adjusting for imports and considering other elements of market structure and behavior, Shepherd (1982) finds substantial increases in industry-level competition from 1958 to 1980. Antitrust policies had the greatest impact in increasing competition, but deregulation and imports were also important.

We can reach quite different conclusions about economic concentration depending on what we look at. For example, Shepherd (1982, p. 621)

Table 4.2   Percentage of Sales Accounted for by Four Largest Producers in Selected Manufacturing Industries, 1947–72

Industry	Percentage of Sales	
	1947	*1972*
Cereal breakfast foods	79	90
Confectionery products	17	32
Chewing gum	70	87
Malt beverages	21	52
Weaving mills, cotton	18[a]	31
Knit underwear mills	21	46
Carpets and rugs	32[b]	78
Men's and boys' suits and coats	9	19
Women's and misses's suits and coats	3[a]	13
Sawmills and planing mills	11[a]	18
Greeting card publishing	39	70
Synthetic rubber	53[a]	62
Flat glass	90[a]	93
Blast furnaces and steel mills	50	45
Cutlery	41	55
Turbines and turbine generators	90[b]	93
Printing trades machinery	31	42
Refrigeration and heating equipment	25	40
Carbon and graphite products	87	80
Household laundry equipment	40	83
Sewing machines	77	84
Electric lamps	92	90
Telephone and telegraph apparatus	90	94[c]
Semiconductors and related devices	46[b]	57
Electronic components	13	36
Primary batteries, dry and wet	76	92
Motor vehicles and car bodies	92[d]	93
Aircraft engines and engine parts	72	77
Locomotives and parts	91	97[d]
Photographic equipment and supplies	61	74
Hard surface floor covering	80	91

Source: Barry Bluestone and Bennett Harrison, *The Deindustrialization of America: Plant Closings, Community Abandonment, and the Dismantling of Basic Industry* (New York: Basic Books, 1982). Adapted from table 5.1, p. 120. Reprinted by permission.
[a]1954 data
[b]1963 data
[c]1970 data
[d]1967 data

considered several industries listed in table 4.2—steel, automobiles, photographic equipment, and sewing machines—to be effectively competitive in 1980, primarily because of increased imports in the 1970s. Other industries, most notably telephone service and equipment, have undergone antitrust actions that have decreased the dominance of one firm. According to Shepherd's estimates, effectively competitive markets accounted for over three-fourths of national income in 1980, an increase of about 25 percent from 1958.

The concentration of economic power within industries is important because it provides freedom from market pressure, allowing concentrated firms direct control over their prices and output. The concentration of economic power within the economy as a whole is also important because it puts decision-making power in fewer hands. The dominance of conglomerate merger activity in recent times has helped increase concentration in the economy. Müller (1977) provides evidence that fewer firms control more of the nation's resources. Between 1955 and 1970, the *Fortune* 500 firms increased their share of profits, assets, and employment in all of U.S. manufacturing and mining by between 40 and 70 percent.

Thus, the United States is experiencing increasing competition within many industries and increasing concentration and centralization across industries. It is difficult to see how workers really benefit from these seemingly contradictory trends. (The trends only appear contradictory. In fact, increased competition, and therefore insecurity, within an industry encourages firms in that industry to diversify by acquiring other firms, spreading their risk.) Despite the increased industrial-level competition in the 1970s, workers' wage increases did not keep pace with inflation and real earnings fell. Meanwhile, merger mania taxed already tight money supplies, increased absentee ownership, and heightened insecurity over jobs among blue- and white-collar employees of firms taken over. Changing patterns of control, technological developments, and capital mobility are intimately related to changes in concentration and centralization.

A firm that can both dictate price, free of market pressure, and restrict output by barring the entry of new firms, is in a position to earn monopoly profits, to control the pace of technological progress, to more closely determine the rate of capital expansion, and to more easily ignore product quality or safety. (Bluestone and Harrison 1982, pp. 119–20)

Control in the Corporation

The large corporation's growth as an economic entity does not necessarily imply an increase in the size of production establishments, commonly measured by number of employees. Yet, in the American experience of manufacturing, the two have gone hand in hand. Increased plant size provided certain economies of scale in goods production. By employing many people in one facility, manufacturers were able to minimize overhead costs, including costs for building and maintaining the facility, and to take advantage of tax incentives frequently provided by communities to large employers. The larger facility enabled firms in certain product areas to move from unit and small-batch production to large-batch and mass production. Standardization of the product and the moving-assembly-line form of organization present in larger production operations led to the replacement of skilled craftsmen with unskilled workers (Averitt 1968).

Economic assets of the larger corporations have enabled some firms to operate the newest type of production, process production. This type of production involves tremendous absolute capital costs, which serve as a barrier to the entry of new firms, and is limited to procedures that can be converted to continuous material flow (liquids, gases, steel, aluminum, and engineering parts are examples). The number of employees involved in process production is likely to be smaller than in mass production where automated machinery does the routine work of the unskilled worker. Skilled workers and highly educated professionals are vital in process production. Averitt (1968) and Blauner (1964) describe these workers in similar ways as highly cooperative and having high morale, beneficiaries of automation rather than victims. But the firm also benefits, since this complex production technique offers high-speed output and low per-unit cost.

Averitt stresses that most firms are usually involved in at least two of these production techniques, though not necessarily in the same plant. However, constraints of these different production types have implications for firm planning and business pricing strategies.

Oligopoly is the natural market structure counterpart to large batch and mass production. When a product is sold under oligopolistic conditions, any initial price decline will likely be followed by all competitors to prevent sales losses to the price cutter; price increases will not be followed by one's competitor unless the initiating firm is the industry price leader and the other firms share a consensus favoring the increase. Administered prices soon become the rule, with the prevailing price commonly set to insure the survival of all reasonably efficient firms. (Averitt 1968, p. 31)

Gordon, Edwards, and Reich (1982) describe the transition from small-batch production to large-batch production as encompassing three dimensions of control: technical, organizational, and social. Their historical examination of labor in the United States identifies three overlapping stages in the social organization of production. (1) A condition of initial proletarianization of the work force occurred between the 1820s and 1890s; (2) homogenization of labor began in the 1870s and terminated during World War II; and (3) a segmented labor force began to emerge in the 1920s and declined in the 1970s. The consolidation of each stage depended on certain institutional innovations that could ensure the basic conditions for capital accumulation. In the first stage, initial proletarianization, a surplus of wage workers was guaranteed by continued immigration and erosion of the economic base of independent farmers and artisans. In the homogenization stage, techniques of management helped break control of skilled workers and rendered ineffectual the opposition of unified workers.

Gordon, Edwards, and Reich claim that by the early 1950s an essentially new structure of labor management was in place in large corporations, aided by the accomodationist impulse of industrial unions. Union contracts negotiated during that time reveal explicit cooperation with the management strategies of corporations: clauses for management rights and productivity bargaining, agreement to unemployment by attrition, and the institutionalization of the grievance procedure. The contracts were not totally made up of concessions by labor, of course. Management's discretion in the allocation of labor was limited by collective bargaining, seniority, and grievance procedures. However, overall, unions gave management control over production in almost every aspect. This contract with labor was also applied by nonunion employers in manufacturing and nonmanufacturing industries, owing to "the coherence of management theory and the similarity of production in many blue-collar and white-collar settings" (Gordon, Edwards, and Reich 1982, p. 189).

The resulting system of labor management reflected the switch from direct intervention by the supervisor to a more bureaucratic form of control in which a full system of rules and procedures operated. A detailed division of jobs and management policy directed technological developments. However, the new systems of labor management were not universally adopted. Only oligopolistic firms could afford them; periphery firms continued to resemble the entrepreneurial firms of the nineteenth century. Thus, after World War II, an identifiable difference in the labor process began to align itself with the differences in corporate structure that had begun to emerge around 1900. This phenomenon occurred in manufacturing and nonmanufacturing industries, although Gordon, Edwards, and Reich argue that in service industries divergence of labor market outcomes takes place as much or more between occupational groupings within industries as between particular sectors. Even core manufacturing firms typically have a segment of their labor force receiving the lower wages and benefits of the secondary labor market.

Although Gordon and his coauthors do not clarify the nature of the labor transformation in the current period, it is clear that the segmentation of the labor force can no longer be assumed to parallel directly the segmentation of the economy into core and periphery firms. They provide the following data on labor market segments of the economy in support of their argument that there has been a trend toward decay of labor-management structure since 1970.

In the subordinate segment of the core, terms of the labor peace, characteristic of the postwar period, no longer hold. Workers in this sector have experienced a reversal in the trend toward rising real wages, employment security, and improving working conditions since the late 1960s. The strategy by corporate management during this period has been to increase the intensity of supervision and management, relocate in nonunion areas nationally and internationally, intensify antiunion activity, and pressure unions for "give-backs" in new contracts.

Independent workers in the core also seem to be experiencing reversals in the implicit bargain they had struck with corporations. The relative earnings differential between independent and subordinate core workers, which had widened from 1950 to 1970, began to close in the 1970s. Opportunities for skill development and relatively autonomous job control have been threatened by a general trend toward routinization of many jobs in this segment. Finally, the combination of stability and advancement sought by workers in this segment in the past now appears elusive as unemployment rates of professional, technical, and managerial workers have risen relative to those of blue-collar workers and as opportunities for college-educated workers to find promising employment have declined.

Because the secondary segment has retained the system of labor management prominent during the labor homogenization stage, it has not experienced the changes in the past decade that the primary sector has experienced. Of all workers, those in this segment have experienced the least decay in wages and working conditions since the early 1970s, largely because conditions in this sector have been so poor all along. Real wages, however, did decline by almost 5 percent between 1973 and 1979.

Gordon, Edwards, and Reich argue that a return to homogenization of labor is unlikely. Instead, the authors foresee a reshuffling of the boundaries of labor market segments and some internal structural changes, but they are not specific about this. Evidence from their study suggests that not all core workers will continue to benefit from the oligopolistic position of their employers. The bifurcation of labor market returns, characteristics of service industries in general, may be increasingly present within core manufacturing and service industries alike. The decline of bureaucratic methods of labor management seems to be met with an increase in technical control over workers at all occupational levels in both manufacturing and service industries of the core.

DESKILLING OF WORK

Closely tied to the issue of worker control is the issue of skill. Postindustrial theories that point to the humanization of work in monopoly capitalism conflict with Marxist theories of the degradation of work in monopoly capitalism. Using census data based on occupational categories to support the postindustrial thesis is thoroughly discredited by Braverman's (1974) historical account of the use of the term *skill* in census classifications. Braverman points out that appearances of an upgrading of the working class from unskilled to semiskilled are an artifact of a change in the occupational scheme used by the Bureau of the Census. Before the 1930s the working class was divided into only two categories, skilled craftsmen and laborers. However, a change in this classification scheme was made to distinguish between laborers who operated machinery and those who did not. The former were called skilled operators and the latter unskilled laborers. Thus, with increasing mechanization of production, the category of the semiskilled grew and that of unskilled laborers declined, even though skills were never actually measured and work involving machines might have been very routine and easily learned.[1]

Scientific Management and Permissive Technologies

Braverman's assessment of the deskilling of American workers points to technological and social forces at work in monopoly capitalism. The technical forces included mechanization and automation, which controlled the pace of work and made workers appendages to machines; routinization of work; and breakdown of skilled tasks into a series of unskilled or less skilled tasks. Accompanying, indeed often dictating and leading, these technical changes was the social organization of production according to Taylor's (1911) principles of scientific management. These principles advocated the use of time-motion studies to set work pace standards. Work was divided so that management controlled knowledge about the logic of production, as well as its technical aspects. The result of these combined forces was a labor force with very little skill; workers became largely interchangeable and adaptable to a large range of simple tasks.

Deskilling is thus presented by Braverman as part of the logic of advanced capitalism, a reflection of a view in which social change results from the struggle between antagonistic social classes. Scientific developments do not arise in a social vacuum, nor is their application—technology—devoid of the class interests of those who control it. Technology may be described as permissive if such developments enable owners and managers to pursue their class interests (Bluestone and Harrison 1982). The permissive technology of the retail industry, represented by computerized cash registers and mass media advertising, led all modes of department stores to adopt similar deskilled sales methods, resulting in a sharp decline in commissioned salespersons (Bluestone et al. 1981).

Technological advances have been accompanied by increased application of the principles of scientific management to the work done by highly trained professionals and technicians. This point, argued well by Braverman (1974), is illustrated by the recent actions of TRW, Inc., a major computer software firm. TRW developed a plan that increased the productivity of its software programmers 39 percent in its first year. The plan involves isolation of technicians in specially designed separate offices, each with its own computer terminal, so that programmers are immediately able to test their designs. Work is individualized and yet monitored through the technical apparatus of the worker. A consultant for TRW stated that "improving white-collar efficiency depends less on structural changes, such as improving the efficiency of machines or layout, than on analyzing how people use their time" (quoted in Brooks 1983, p. 33). Cost of the investment, estimated at about $10,000 per worker, is prohibitive to firms without oligopolistic or conglomerate resources available to them.

Consequences for Workers

The result of deskilling in core manufacturing firms did not have negative consequences for workers' earnings as long as unions were able to negotiate for a share of the gains from increased productivity. However, service industries encompass workers at the extremes of the skill continuum; those in what have been regarded as low-skill occupations have traditionally earned low wages while professionals, technicians, and managers have been highly rewarded. Braverman (1974) argues that the advance of technologically oriented occupations results in a shrinkage of the labor force concentrated in those areas and in a concomitant increase in the labor-intensive areas that have not yet been or cannot be subjected to high technology. The latter areas have traditionally been the province of the competitive sector of the economy, including large parts of service industries. The share of employment in the periphery should be increased with technological advances, although, as Sullivan (1981) notes, workers in service occupations may be easily integrated into firms of all types and monopolies on services are prototypical of many primary-sector firms. Thus, growth in the share of employment in the periphery need not keep pace with growth in the service sector.

Future high-growth jobs in the United States have been projected to be in the very areas where technology is not available to mechanize or where availability of a low-cost labor force has made mechanization unprofitable, such as janitorial and hospital aide work (see Carey 1981). Education-intensive white-collar jobs are not expanding at the rate of the labor force available to do them; as many as 20 percent of college graduates will be victims of occupational mismatch in the 1980s (Young and Hayghe 1984). Blue-collar jobs in core firms are declining, partly because of mechanization and partly because of the capital flight from the United States to the Third World, where a cooperative, low-cost labor force exists.[2]

The Bureau of Labor Statistics expects lower-level white-collar jobs, often referred to as pink-collar jobs because of the predominance of women in these positions, to grow at a rate slightly above the national average through 1990 (Carey 1981). However, automation and capital flight may slow the growth of clerical positions more than previously thought (see Reskin and Hartmann 1986, p. 33; and *Business Week* 1986, p. 81). For example, the growth rate for secretarial jobs will probably decline as word processors become standard office equipment. In this area, deskilling and reskilling are occurring as secretaries learn to operate desktop computers and simultaneously find that skills of spelling and setting format can be handled by the computer. Further, complaints are common of back pains, headaches, and eye strain from eight-hour days spent on these machines in offices not properly designed for the new technology. Working conditions have, in many ways, worsened (see Glenn and Feldberg 1979).

The growth of service industries also suggests that skill requirements will be more sharply divided among available jobs. Expansion of the education-intensive segment of the service industry seems to have slowed considerably in the 1970s and will probably continue to do so in the 1980s as opportunities for employment in the public sector decline. Movement from lower to upper level in services is extremely restricted. Stanback and Noyelle (1982) note that upward mobility in services is dependent on a change of industry, not jobs. This situation becomes unlikely in a tight job market, such as that which characterized the early 1980s.

Technological developments of mechanical and social varieties accompanying the increased physical and economic scale of firms have led to a general loss of skill among workers. This occurrence has not always resulted in lower wages, especially in core manufacturing firms. However, changes in the ability of core workers to demand greater economic returns may now place deskilled workers in a position comparable to that of their counterparts in the periphery. This tendency has been furthered by another important structural change in worker power, the mobility of capital.

MOBILITY OF CAPITAL

Bluestone and Harrison (1982) described the changing industrial structure of the United States in the postwar period, which postindustrial theorists see as part of the evolutionary process of societal development, as the result of widespread, systematic disinvestment in the nation's basic productive capacity. This process of disinvestment, labeled *deindustrialization*, has extreme consequences for workers and communities in which plant closings occur. One-third of displaced workers experience long-term unemployment and, when reemployed, commonly experience declines in occupational status and earnings. Women and older men are much more likely than men in their prime to get jobs in the secondary sector after losing jobs in the core. But there are also ripple effects outside the community in which a plant closes. Bluestone and Harrison estimate that for every 100 jobs lost in the auto industry, 105 jobs are lost in the direct supplier network, and substantial job losses are also experienced in nonmanufacturing areas such as transportation and warehouses, wholesale and retail trade, and business services.

Corporate Strategy

According to Bluestone and Harrison (1982), capital is more mobile because of concentration in corporate structure and a "new managerialism" emphasizing cash management over product line. From 1946 to 1971, merger activity made large corporations even larger; the resulting absentee ownership meant corporations had few ties to communities. Labor unions were primarily concerned with improving wages and working conditions, leaving companies free to make the larger decisions of production and investment unhampered by labor demands. Furthermore, unions were not making gains in organizing new members; regions of the country remained nonunionized, providing a haven for runaway shops. Overall, corporate strategy reflected the growing need for flexibility, and flexibility depended on the availability of cash.

Corporate strategy was reflected in increased concentration of the postwar U.S. economy and centralization of control by fewer and fewer firms. Merger activity was motivated in part by corporate need for cash. The easing of government regulations and restrictions covering merger activity during certain historical periods reinforced corporate tendencies toward centralization. Capital centralization was accompanied by growth of "unproductive" workers—managers, technicians, and other types of administrative workers—within manufacturing and nonmanufacturing firms. Whole industries arose to meet the needs of larger and more complex corporations. These industries grew tremendously during the postwar period. (Stanback et al. [1981] estimate that 25 percent of the Gross National Product originates from intermediate producer services, those used either in goods production or in getting goods to the purchasers.)

All of these trends combined in the 1950s and 1960s to produce high growth and U.S. dominance of the world economy. But their culmination led to the decline of U.S. hegemony by 1970, what Blumberg (1980) calls "the end of the American century." This decline has led to an increased emphasis on making U.S. goods competitive in the world market, especially through fighting labor unions. Periphery industries avoid unions by moving plants to nonunion territory, such as rural areas or the Sun Belt, when unionization threatens. Core industries, such as automobiles and electrical goods, have developed elaborate systems of parallel production and multiple sourcing—the operation of multistate, multiregional, and multinational systems of plants and subcontractors. This strategy diminishes the capacity of a strike in one plant to shut down the whole production operation. Plants are increasingly located in states having right-to-work laws that free shops from requiring union membership of all workers even when a majority of workers vote for unionization. Consulting firms in the business of helping companies avoid unionization are developing rapidly.

Bluestone and Harrison (1982) believe management's antiunion response will be ineffective in reducing labor costs in any significant long-term way because so few U.S. workers belong to unions. The corporate need for flexibility has been channeled into an attack on the social wage, which is seen as a disincentive to working for low wages. The social wage, represented by social welfare programs, including unemployment insurance, varies from state to state but tends to be highest in the "antibusiness" states of the North. Capital mobility is putting pressure on every part of the country for a reduction in the social wage. If a nationwide reduction should occur, Bluestone and Harrison reason that the standard of living of all workers will decline because the power of labor, unionized or not, will decline.

The mobility of capital, therefore, may have consequences for workers across the nation, through the general attack on the welfare state and the specific actions taken by corporations to preserve flexibility. The most mobile corporations are likely to be in the core sector of the economy.

In highly concentrated industries the control over capital location and therefore jobs is wielded by a small set of decision makers. If one or even several firms in an unconcentrated industry decides to move, that decision will usually have minimal consequences for the industry's total labor force. Yet a single decision by one corporate board in a concentrated industry can . . . affect the livelihood of thousands of workers and the stability of entire communities. . . . As in the case of concentrated manufacturing ownership, narrowing control over key nonmanufacturing sectors of the economy brings an increasing tendency toward monopoly pricing, restricted output, political influence, and centralized control over capital location. (Bluestone and Harrison 1982, p. 121)

Services: An Exception?

Some analysts have suggested that services, by their nature, are immobile, unlikely to leave local markets because they cannot be stockpiled or shipped or because they may be bound by geographical licensing (Sullivan 1981). While personal, social, and consumer services might fit these restrictions, other services, especially producer services, tend to be as footloose as nonservice industries.

Dogged by the same competitive pressures that face manufacturers, managers are scanning the globe for cheaper labor. . . . So far, it's only the low value-added jobs that are being shipped out. Data entry and clerical work are the natural candidates. Fear that these jobs will be eliminated by outsourcing or automation leads Executive Director Karen Nussbaum of 9 to 5, a national association of working women, to predict that clerical employees will make up "the next generation of dislocated workers." (*Business Week* 1986, p. 81)

The permissive technologies of telecommunications, rapid transportation, and information management systems are freeing service industries from their ties to localities. It is becoming increasingly possible to ship information and stockpile services. Restrictions on geographical licensing are subject to change with the prevailing political winds, currently blowing toward corporate freedom.

The banking industry represents a good example of the changes permissive technologies are bringing to service industries. Geographical restrictions have been transcended despite the illegality of interstate banking. Banks do own each other, and banking operations extend across state boundaries through a system that allows customers of member banks to use any bank in the system. Automated teller machines and bank cards have facilitated the "shipping" of banking services across the nation, and programming these machines to provide a range of services has allowed many routine banking operations to be "stockpiled" until the demand exists. The closing of many small-town banks has forced customers to go the provider rather than the other way around.

Service industries can also take advantage of economies of scale, despite the limits localities place on market size. If the firm operates on a multiunit basis, as many producer and consumer services do, firm size will not be restricted by size of local markets; only the size of the establishment will be so limited. Service firms may also use transportation and communication advancements to expand market size. Sears Roebuck and Company rose to dominance in the retail industry through its mail-order business, which opened a national market in an industry characterized as small-scale and localized. Sears has used its dominance in retailing to enter other service industries, including real estate, insurance, finance, and stock brokerage and investments. Thus, economies of scale are brought in by the parent firm, and delivery of a broad range of services can be achieved on a national scale by using existing resources.

Transformation to a service-based economy will probably not result in any dramatic changes in the power of capital to determine its location.

Furthermore, it must be remembered that service industries tend to be closely related to manufacturing industries in function and location. As white-collar labor is deskilled, service industries will not be bound to a particular region by the availability of a highly educated work force. The close ties between manufacturing and services that aid in production and distribution mean that loss of jobs in the former sector has reverberations in the service sector as well. The deindustrialization of America is a broad-ranging experience likely to be felt by workers in all industries.

The institutional arrangements of segmentation are being replaced by new forms of organization. Production is being organized in the 1970s and 1980s by a resurgence of technical control accomplished through permissive technologies, and workers' resources are being limited by the mobility of capital. The evidence suggests a new period of proletarianization, a reduction in labor segmentation along industry sectoral lines, and an increase in inequality based on class position. Transformation within the dual economy has considerably reduced the protections and privileges afforded core workers. The loss of manufacturing establishments has reduced medium-pay job opportunities and has created, by default, a service economy.

SUMMARY: CHANGING RESOURCES AND OUTCOMES

Although closely intertwined, control, skill, and mobility can be considered separate resources available to those contending for power in the work setting. Control, as a resource for owners, refers to the ability to determine the type of work done, its allocation and execution by workers. Corporate control over technology, especially mechanization, has led to considerable control over the pace of work and product quality. Technical control by owners has advanced steadily in almost every area of production, from fast-food establishments to automobile assembly plants. For example, McDonald's restaurants use timers for deep fryers, measured servings for soft drink dispensers, and product-coded keys on computerized cash registers to minimize worker skill and error.

Technical skill allows workers to gain advantage in the class struggle if they can ensure that the skill remains in demand of if they can regulate its supply. Craft unions and licensing and accreditation procedures (advanced degrees and professional schools) help regulate the supply of skilled workers, but generally workers have been unable to prevent the obsolescence of their skills or to guarantee access to new skills through retraining. Braverman (1974) describes the deskilling of occupations in monopoly capitalism as a progressive phenomenon touching not just blue-collar occupations but also white-collar work. Capitalists use technological advances in machinery to reduce workers' skills and the power of workers to ensure a sufficient market for their skills.

The result has been a shift in employment opportunity from production arenas that have undergone mechanization to labor-intensive jobs, such as those in the service sector. Job losses in manufacturing in the 1980 to 1982 period have been estimated at two million positions, and the majority (85 percent) of new jobs created in the 1980s are expected to come in services (Karmin et al. 1984). Within manufacturing, the more labor-intensive operations of the periphery sector gain relative to the core. "Over the past decade, TRW's employment has risen from 80,000 to 85,000, while its purchasing of goods and services has generated an estimated 25,000 jobs among its suppliers" (Karmin et al. 1984, p. 42).

Material technology, therefore, has been a major advantage to capitalists in areas of control and skill. Social technologies of organization also have been an important component of capitalist control and the deskilling of workers. Organizing work along lines of scientific management has had the effect of fragmenting tasks to less skilled components, facilitating overall deskilling of the work force. In scientific management, time-motion studies determine the proper procedure and pace of work appropriate to the task. This social technology has increased capitalist control over the execution of work but has not been the only important mechanism available in the struggle for control.

As the size of corporations has grown, so has the need to control decision making and allocate supervisory responsibility. The bureaucratic hierarchical structure allows control over production workers and administrative personnel in the enterprise. The hierarchical structure remains the hallmark of corporate and government organizations and is central to the proletarianization of U.S. society. Proletarianization means that control over the process of production, as well as its purposes, has been taken from the worker. Autonomy in work is replaced by subordination. Subordination, typical of blue-collar and lower white-collar employment, appears increasingly in professional and technical positions (Wright and Singelmann 1982). Proletarianization also results from loss of self-employment in the work force, a development parallel to loss of small business in the United States.

The bureaucratic organization of work also entails formalization of hiring and promotion procedures and rationalization of negotiations over wages and benefits. Internal job ladders and collective bargaining work to the advantage of workers and have been especially prevalent in union-dominated industries. Just as large size has enabled corporations to afford the material technology of mechanization and the social technology of scientific management, the industry of employment has become important to workers, enabling them to benefit from bureaucratic organization. As unions lose power, worker ability to bargain successfully for wage and benefit packages declines. Concessions made by unions in the business recession of 1980 to 1983 show that union control over working conditions and wages is diminishing. In 1982, unionized workers in private industry received only a 3.8 percent increase in their wages for the first year of their labor contracts, down from the 9.8 percent agreed on in collective bargaining in 1981 (U.S. Department of Labor 1985, p. 332). Average wage adjustments continued to decline to a record low of 2.3 percent in 1985 (U.S. Department of Labor 1986, p. 85).

Career mobility is also being restricted by shortening internal job ladders. Workers are unable to advance very far in positions of responsibility and skill without being placed in competition with persons from outside the establishment. Stanback and Noyelle (1982) note that production and nonproduction workers of the same manufacturing company often work in different buildings, removed from each other in a physical as well as in a career sense. Service workers improve their positions primarily by changing industries. The result of this reduction in career ladders is a loss of semiskilled occupations and a consequent polarization of skilled and unskilled workers in services and in manufacturing.

Finally, geographic mobility can be considered a resource in the class struggle. Capital mobility has advantages that far outstrip those of labor mobility. Workers are free to pursue employment opportunities anywhere within national boundaries but not internationally. They are unlikely, however, to have access to information regarding availability of jobs suited to their skills and are likely to be forced to give up wage benefits and retirement protections accrued through seniority. Workers displaced from employment in the core sector tend to face work under different conditions in the nonunion regions of the country where employment opportunities are expanding. Workers have less access to the money needed for geographic mobility than do capitalists, and they are likely to face a reduction in their standing of living, even if wages are not lowered, if they must sell homes with low-interest mortgages and obtain housing at higher market prices. Thus, workers are severely constrained in their ability to follow capital or pursue new employment.

Capital has legal and financial advantages over workers in its movement. Establishments can close in one location and relocate virtually wherever they choose without obligations to their old community or nation. The United States is unique in the industrialized world in this freedom (Blumberg 1980). Large corporations can gain tax advantages from lost capital in closed plants and have ample access to the capital needed to shift operations or open new facilities. Filing for bankruptcy and reorganization can enable firms to break union contracts and reopen in the same facility, giving them the effect of movement without movement. International competition for the jobs in the core has accompanied the expansion of the international activities of core firms. If the multinational firm expands its operations outside the United States, jobs within the United States are threatened. Unions must make concessions or face plant closings. The core firm may not suffer from international competition; the core industry probably will.

All of these changes in the resources available to workers and capital will affect the outcomes of their struggle. Whereas most of the post–World War II period has been characterized by rising real income for workers, the 1970s brought losses in real earnings to many categories of workers (Blumberg 1980). Changes in control, skill, and mobility since 1960 suggest a worsening of conditions for the most vulnerable workers in the 1980s: older workers and younger workers.

NOTES

1. This point continues to be missed. In Form's (1983) critical review of sociological research on the American working class, deskilling is examined as one of the four themes of Braverman's work. However, Form uses the census data discredited by Braverman to try to discredit Braverman's argument.

2. More than three-fourths of the jobs lost between July 1981 and December 1982 were in manufacturing, especially in factories involving the production of durable goods (English and DeLouise 1983).

5
Data and Decisions Regarding Analysis

New structuralists have argued that returns to workers depend not just on the skills they possess but also on the economic sector in which they obtain employment. The dualism in the advanced capitalist form of production has created differences within the working class that are manifested in average earnings for workers and in the age-earnings relationship. These differences appear to be static, reflecting stability in the dual economic structure (Hodson 1978). From this perspective, economic segmentation is an outcome, not a process. What the new structuralist approach has missed is the ongoing nature of transformation, a transformation within the dualist organization of production. Conversely, the technical functional approach has failed to grasp the structure in which the technological changes in production occur. The interaction of the two processes may indeed best explain the changing returns to workers since 1960.

Without a doubt, there has been a transformation in this century of the manpower needs of production. As technical functionalists have pointed out, employment in distributive, producer, and social service sectors has increased at the expense of employment, first in the extractive sector and recently in the transformative sector. New structuralists point to a transformation of the forms of production, a transformation which has led to the development of oligopolistic and competitive capital sectors. To some extent, technical functionalist and new structuralist views of the transformation coincide. Hodson (1978) points out that the monopoly sector is composed primarily of manufacturing and mining industries; service and distributive industries provide the primary opportunities for competitive sector employment. Likewise, Stanback et al. (1981) argue that development of a service economy has produced changes in the earnings structure, creating a dichotomy of good and bad jobs. Typically, employment in the transformative sector has tended toward the middle earnings categories. However, in the service sector more workers are found in the higher and lower earnings categories and fewer in the middle categories. Neither approach to social change and the resulting systems of stratification has adequately accounted for the changes in social organization suggested by the opposing view. In this chapter, I outline my approach to the study of age, earnings, and change in the U.S. economy.

WHO, WHAT, AND WHEN?

To assess changes in the structure of employment and its outcomes for workers, we need to look at a period of time that characterizes the relevant changes in the economy. For this purpose, I have chosen 1960 as the baseline, since it is at this point that the service sector began to grow at the expense of the transformative sector, marking the beginning of the "new" economy (Singelmann 1978). I will compare the situation in 1960 with that of 1980. Broad descriptive data on employment in capital and industrial sectors provide some understanding of the conditions guiding labor force participation in each period. Individual-level data on earnings and employment conditions allow analysis of earnings inequality along the lines of age, sex, and economic sector. The issues suggested by human capital and dual economy theories can therefore be addressed through analysis of a large sample of workers containing social, economic, and demographic information.

Data and Sample

The person records from the public use files of the U.S. Census of Population and Housing for 1960 and for 1980 (A sample), one-in-a-thousand sample size, meet the considerations outlined above. The study populations comprise civilians aged 14 and older in 1960 and 16 and older in 1980 who were gainfully employed in the year preceding the census (1959 and 1979) and who were in nonextractive industries during the reference week of the census year or during the last employment period (since 1949 for the 1960 census and since 1975 for the 1980 census). Civilians included employees in private-sector industries and federal, state, and local government workers; the self-employed were not included. The extractive industries of agriculture, fishing, forestry, and mining were excluded because growth in employment in service industries since 1960 has come at the expense of transformative industry employment rather than at the expense of extractive industries, as occurred prior to 1960 (Singelmann 1978). Furthermore, the processes of production and major occupational categories in extractive industries are qualitatively different from those in other industries. The exclusion of extractive industries does not substantially affect comparability with previous applications of the dual economy model, since the percentage of labor force in question is small and evenly divided between periphery (agriculture, forestry, and fishing) and core (mining).

Comparability of Data

The best laid plans of researchers can be foiled by the periodic updating of measures in the U.S. census. A major complication in the comparability of 1960 and 1980 census data comes with use of the occupation variable. The changing U.S. economic structure has led to the addition, reclassification, and elimination of many occupational categories, and the Census Bureau advises caution in interpreting changes associated with occupation. One way to minimize the amount of bias that might be introduced with an occupation variable is to use a very broad categorical measure rather than attempting a hierarchical ordering of specific occupations. I focus on the effect of employment in managerial, professional, and technical occupations in keeping with Stanback and Noyelle's (1982) suggestion of a "new segmentation" between these workers and all others. Theoretical interest in the bifurcation of the labor market provides ample justification for categorizing occupation so broadly. This categorization should reduce considerably the problems associated with changes in occupation codes.

Other variables affected by changes in measurement or classification by the Census Bureau are age and earnings. In 1960, labor force data were supplies for persons aged 14 and older. In 1980, 16 was the lower age limit. My consideration of age categories (less than 25, 25 to 34, 35 to 44, 45 to 54, 55 to 64, 65 and over) makes this change of minimal concern. The youngest age group I consider contains such a variety of work orientations at both times that the exclusion of 14- and 15-year-olds in 1980 should not affect the ability to draw conclusions about this age group. All conclusions will be necessarily limited by the work character of the age group.

Earnings are coded with more precision in 1980 than in 1960 census data, and the constant dollar values of the highest category differ. Thus, the decision to use constant dollars involves some imprecision. Converting 1959 earnings to 1979 dollars would have put all incomes greater than $25,000 in the single category of $62,500, although the 1980 census reported incomes through $75,000. Converting 1979 earnings to 1959 dollars results in the loss of differentiation of incomes between $62,500 and $75,000, which would fall into the single 1960 category for incomes of $25,000 and higher. The latter method is used because it improves the comparability of the earnings variable.

Earnings are given for the year preceding the census. Industry and occupation, however, are current for the census year. The analysis of earnings associated with occupation and industry, therefore, is based on the assumption of continuity of employment between the census year and the one preceding it. This assumption is necessary in 1960 because no information on industry or occupation for the earnings year is available. Although labor market information of this type is available in the 1980 census, the information pertaining to the census year is used to make the assumptions between the two data sets as similar as possible.

SEGMENTATION: CAPITAL AND INDUSTRIAL

The development of monopoly capitalism has transformed the production process in its ownership and management patterns (organizational structure), market concentration, economic size, and technical system of production (Averitt 1968). Accompanying the growth of monopoly capitalism has been a change in the type of productive activity within the United States. This phenomenon has been generally referred to as the growth of the service economy (Fuchs 1968), which has steadily increased its share of the labor force in this century (Singelmann 1978). The effect of these developments on the resources of workers and capitalists has been the subject of the theoretical debates outlined in previous chapters. The task at hand is to assess the nature of changing resources through discovery of the changing outcomes of labor force participation. To accomplish this task, we must control for the effect of industrial segmentation and capital segmentation on earnings.

Making Economic Structure Understandable

Critiques of the dual economy formulations have appeared in the major sociological journals since sociologists first began to systematize and quantify the dimensions of industrial structure discussed by Averitt in 1968. Despite the critiques, researchers have clung to one or another of the standard formulations (commonly used are Hodson [1978] and Tolbert, Beck, and Horan [1980]). The idea of separate structures appeals to the sociological search for clarity. Certainly, reality is more complex than empirical studies can ever capture; social scientists must always walk the fine line between oversimplifying and overspecifying their models. Both situations lead away from adequate understanding of social reality, in the first case by omission, in the latter by commission.

The search to understand economic structures involves these same dilemmas. How many segments do we need to explain earnings, unemployment, underemployment? Two? Three? Four? Six? Fourteen? And of what are these segments composed? Firms? Establishments? Industries? Jobs? The answers to these questions are often derived empirically (see Hodson 1983), but the questions are conceptual, too. In our search for understanding of economic structure and changing resources of workers and employers, we can use an existing dualist model, modifying it slightly to bring out an important aspect of production—the type of industry.

Industry as Level of Segmentation

Does industry, company, or workplace constitute the meaningful structure workers encounter? Here, too, controversy abounds. One way to resolve the dispute is to acknowledge that each level is important in its own way and that the problem is not to decide which is best but to determine how each operates to empower or to control workers. While agreeing with this reasoning, I contend that industries have appeal beyond the availability and comparability of data (although these advantages are considerable, especially for a historical focus). This appeal is theoretical.

In focusing on class resources and outcomes for workers, we need to look at commonalities in the work experience. An industry is characterized by firms that share a product market; it is at the level of the product market that firms and nations compete. If an industry is highly price competitive—the airline industry, for example—workers will be affected differently than if there is little competition—as with breakfast cereals. Some industries face competitive pressures from abroad, but U.S. firms in a given industry may not be hurt if they have made arrangements with their overseas competition. The U.S. tire industry provides a good example of such industry-level competition. Goodyear Tire and Rubber is linked to its foreign competition through technology sales to Bridgestone of Japan and through manufacturing arrangements with Dunlop of Britain. To complete the picture, Goodyear is involved in a joint venture with Michelin of France (Bluestone and Harrison 1982). Another U.S. tire company, Firestone Tire and Rubber, turned red ink into black by selling its radial truck-tire plant to Bridgestone and buying tires made in their old plant (*Business Week* 1986). Thus, while international competition in the tire industry may hurt U.S. workers, U.S. firms may not be affected in the same way.

Import competition indirectly affects workers in the industries on both sides of the production process of the market directly affected. For each $1 billion of foreign-made autos, $1.2 billion is lost in auto production; $778 million in manufacture of steel, machine tools, and other materials; $348 million in distribution industries; $47 million in mining; $39 million in finance and insurance; and $16 million in plant construction (*Business Week* 1986, p. 62).

In addition to product market similarities, industries have similar labor market characteristics. Industrial specialization brings labor specialization. The machines workers use or tend are similar within industrial classifications. Changes within an industry affect the types of jobs and numbers of workers in those jobs. A push within an industry to lower production costs is likely to affect workers through changes in the labor market. White-collar employees, for example, find their positions cut back even in healthy firms. Corporate loyalty is eroding, leading one worker in biotechnology to state, "We are all gypsies. . . . You work for an industry, not a company" (quoted in Nussbaum et al. 1986, p. 44).

The world of blue-collar workers offers more familiar examples of industry effects on labor. The textile industry, feeling the pinch of cheap foreign labor and a strong U.S. dollar, sought to lower its labor costs in the 1980s by automating. Between 1975 and 1982, the industry spent $6.8 billion on new machines and upgraded factories; labor costs dropped from 30 percent to less than 20 percent of total production costs. In the early 1970s, more than one million people were employed in textile mills; in 1983, there were about 750,000 (Flagg 1983, p. 2D). Workers in many industries have been powerless to save jobs from automation; the best they can do is make retraining and employment security a priority in contract negotiations with employers in declining or cyclical industries (automobiles and steel).

Stories of laid-off workers in declining industries and of high unemployment levels in their communities and states illustrate another important feature of industries—their regional nature. Automobile production has been concentrated in the North Central region, textiles in the Southeast, and microelectronics in the Northeast and in California. This regional concentration has had the consequence of reducing the options of workers when cutbacks or layoffs occur. A plant closing by a major employers in a community throws many people with similar skills and experience out into a labor market unable to absorb them. This is true of blue-collar and white-collar industries. Unemployment of steelworkers in Youngstown, Ohio, and Pittsburgh, Pennsylvania, gained national attention in the early 1980s, but so did the loss of high-tech jobs in Silicon Valley, California. The decline of a regionally concentrated industry or the closing of a major employer in a community has a multiplier effect, which makes it even more difficult to find employment or to sell one's home to move and get a job elsewhere. Workers look for jobs in similar industries; they do not expect to be transferred to different industrial subsidiaries of their former employer.

Finally, industries represent meaningful aggregates of workers because production of goods or services is carried out within industries. Firms represent legal units, not necessarily production units. In a special issue focusing on the loss of manufacturing in the United States, *Business Week* (March 3, 1986) decried "hollow corporations," which serve not as producers but as distribution agents of goods from overseas. Some of these companies are almost exclusively involved in marketing, using external suppliers and having only a small central headquarters. Nike, an athletic apparel company, had $1 billion in revenues in 1985, but only 100 of its 3,500 employees were involved in manufacturing. Ocean Pacific Sunwear, an apparel company, represents an even more extreme case. In 1985, the firm had revenues of $15 million and only 67 employees, none in manufacturing. Furthermore, whereas firm ownership can change rapidly and can be difficult to trace, there is a constancy about industries (even given the changing of industrial classification codes) that makes them attractive for the study of social change.

The Model of Economic Segmentation

Classification of economic sectors for 1960 and 1980 data is accomplished by use of Tolbert, Horan, and Beck's schema of core and periphery industries. The theoretical framework for their classification scheme is similar to mine in that it interprets "economic segmentation as a contextual factor, which operates in such a way as to condition the effects of basic socioeconomic processes on individual workers" (Tolbert, Horan, and Beck 1980, p. 1106). They use three types of empirical indicators of industrial structure: (1) measures of market concentration and economic scale, (2) measures of oligopolistic behavior in the industrial product market (especially profit), and (3) measures of the relative size of the bureaucratic work force and the extent of internal labor market development.

The latter of these measures is the most controversial theoretically and is the major discrepancy between their model and that of other new structuralists, who argue that labor market and economic structure should be kept conceptually distinct. Hodson and Kaufman (1981) charge that the inclusion of labor market variables in dual economy classifications introduces circularity and tautological reasoning into studies employing such classifications to study labor market outcomes. In rebuttal,

Horan, Tolbert, and Beck (1981) seek support in the large body of litera-ture dealing with the ecological fallacy issue. They argue that incorpor-ation of aggregate individual characteristics into indexes of industrial structure does not prohibit examination of individual outcomes. Further-more, use of a schema that includes labor market measures strengthens my examination of the changing nature of economic segmentation. If I find different labor market returns associated with economic sector in 1980 than in 1960 despite incorporation of labor market variables in the classification index, then the assumed parallelism between labor market and economic sectors is called into question.

There is a problem in using a classification scheme derived since 1960 but not as recently as 1980 for analysis of data from these two times. The complexity involved in empirically defining structure according to speci-fications of the theory has discouraged researchers from redefining the structures when looking across time. Noting the lack of adequate histori-cal data for an empirical study of social class, Wright and Singelmann (1982) could only estimate social class membership for 1960 and 1970. This estimation involved applying information from a 1969 survey to population census data.

This procedure involves an assumption, which, according to the theory ad-vanced in this paper, is probably incorrect—namely, that the class distributions within occupations (within economic sectors) remained unchanged during the decade, and thus such a distribution in 1969 could be used to estimate the class structure from census data for 1960. . . . Because of these problems in estimating the class structure, we felt that it was not feasible to carry the analysis back in time to the 1950 census. Whatever distortions occurred in imputing the class structure to 1960 would have been greatly exaggerated for earlier periods. (1982, p. 193)

Freedman (1976) faced similar difficulties in her use of occupation-in-dustry matrices for 1960 and 1970 to compare labor market earnings segments. Although exact replication of positions was impossible, Freedman's approach to generating labor market segments, via their earnings similarities, allowed her to define 1960 and 1970 sectors with a high degree of similarity. Researchers who prefer to define their eco-nomic structures conceptually and study their effect on the earnings process across time will not be able to use Freedman's approach.

The time problem is not prohibitive in my study, since data sources for the variables Tolbert, Horan, and Beck (1980) used cut across a wide swath of the 1960 to 1980 period (see table 5.1), ranging from 1966 (four-firm adjusted concentration ratio) to 1976 (earnings data). If eco-nomic concentration within industries decreased from 1960 to 1980 (Shepherd 1982), the effect of the application of Tolbert, Horan, and Beck's categories to 1960 and 1980 census data might be a slight under-estimation of the core in 1960 and a slight overestimation in 1980. The application of static classification schemes to the study of economic change is not ideal but does serve the intent of exploration into changes occurring within the economic structure.

Table 5.1   Variables Tolbert, Horan, and Beck Used to Derive Economic Sectors

Mean corporate expenditure on advertising (1972)
Mean assets of corporations (1972)
Four-firm adjusted concentration ratio (1966)
Mean fringe benefit expenditure per worker (1972)
Mean hourly wage of production and nonsupervisory workers (1976; adjusted to 1972 dollars)
Median annual income of workers (1969; adjusted to 1972 dollars)
Mean political contributions (1972)
Mean profit (or net income) of business units (1972)
Proportion of supervisory or nonproduction personnel (1976)
Proportion of unionized workers (1970)
Proportion of workers working 50 to 52 weeks per year (1969)
Mean number of voluntary or involuntary terminations per 100 workers (1976)
Mean business receipts (1972)
Median years employed with same firm for males (1972)
Mean hours worked per week by production and nonsupervisory personnel (1976)
Mean weekly wage for production and nonsupervisory personnel (1976)
Mean number of workers per business unit (1970)

Source: Charles M. Tolbert II, Patrick M. Horan, and E. M. Beck, "The Structure of Economic Segmentation," *American Journal of Sociology* 85 (1980). Adapted from table 1, p. 1100. Reprinted with permission.

The industries in the 1960 and 1980 censuses were assigned to the sectors that Tolbert, Horan, and Beck reported for the 1970 census. The classification of industries is reported in appendix A with an indication of the 1960, 1970, and 1980 census codes and the allocation of industries coded or defined differently in 1960 or 1980 than in 1970.

Sharpening the Focus: Industrial Categories

The other transformation of interest in the productive process involves the what of production. The rise of service industries has meant that a greater share of employment is found in industries concerned with providing a service rather than with transforming raw materials into finished goods. Although the varieties of services these industries provide are great, ranging from financial to personal, and although there are historical changes in the importance of particular types of services

(Singelmann 1978), I consider only two categories of industrial production: transformative and service. These categories are based on definitions developed by Browning and Singelmann (1978). The transformative sector comprises the construction industry, manufacturing, and utilities, and the service sector includes transportation, communications, wholesale and retail trade, producer services, social services, and personal services. The industrial designation of the industries from the 1960 and 1980 censuses are indicated along with capital sector designation in appendix A.

Focusing on the type of industry—transformative or service—improves the dualist model because it helps capture some of the complexity of economic structure but does so with categories we can easily understand. The industrial-sector distinction is not primarily technological in nature—service-sector workers often deal with machinery of one type or another, whether it be computers, cash registers, wrenches, or floor buffers—nor is it primarily a distinction of occupation, since transformative industries employ a variety of workers in service-type occupations. Of course, there is a considerable overlap between the industrial-sector distinction and the representation of broad occupational groups. Most sales workers are in the service sector; most craftsmen are in the transformative sector. Both sectors employ managers, technicians, and other professionals.

The distinction between industrial sectors is important because it helps sharpen the focus on class resources. Houghland (1985) found industry category more useful than capital sector in explaining wages of a select group of workers. Service and transformative industries differ in establishment size, unionization, geographical location, governmental regulation, and ownership structure (franchises and holding companies are more common in service industries). These differences have been prominent in the past and have been important for workers. Combined with the capital-sector distinction from economic dualism, the industrial-sector distinction can help us see where the important changes in production are occurring. This should also aid in theoretical refinement of the new structuralist perspective, since most of the dualist historiography and its critiques have been based on a model of manufacturing industries. With services playing an increasingly prominent role in employment, the analytical separation of service and transformative industries in the core and periphery is interesting from a practical and theoretical perspective.

CHANGING OUTCOMES: EARNINGS IN THE SEGMENTED ECONOMY

Although the heart of the theoretical debate presented in previous chapters centers on the dynamics of change in capitalist industrial society, the data available to study these changes tap only the effects of the transformation. Earnings represent an outcome of the structural changes in the how and the what of production. The changing resources available to workers and capitalists in the postwar period appear to have weakened the position of formerly powerful groups of workers. Earnings should reflect this change. Rather than homogenization and convergence in economic returns, the evidence from some new structuralists (Gordon, Edwards, and Reich 1982; Stanback and Noyelle 1982) seems to suggest a growing divergence within the working class between those in a few select occupations and the rest of the workers. The benefits of oligopolistic structure will be less accessible to all core workers, and the declining power of these workers will be experienced first and most keenly by the most vulnerable age groups, the young and the old.

Age and Inequality

My study deviates markedly from other new structuralist studies in my emphasis on age, not as an indicator of experience or stamina, but as a correlate of power. This does not fit into a theory of aging but a theory of advantage. I have argued in earlier chapters that age, considered important in functional theories of stratification, can help new structuralists understand better the structure of reward and theorize about the structure of power. To the extent that new structuralists have limited their interpretation of age to that of the technical functionalists, they have missed the importance of the relative position of age groups to each other. If age is considered a proxy for work experience, as it commonly is in studies using census data, the analysis of age-related earnings is problematic.

The most obvious problem is the computation of experience (most commonly, age minus six years of childhood minus the years of schooling equals years of experience) because of its assumptions of immediate, and more or less permanent, employment after schooling ends. This formula is believed most valid for white males and least valid for white females, now nearly half of all workers (see Farley 1984). Given the high unemployment rates of black males since 1970, the use of age as a proxy for work experience will become increasingly problematic for this labor force group.

The other problem in using age to compute experience lies in the lack of information on the industry or occupation in which the experience was acquired. In theory, experience is important to employers because it provides the opportunity to improve skills. Workers in the secondary labor market receive lower rewards for experience than do those in the primary sector for two reasons: (1) the skills required take little time to develop, and (2) their work experience is less likely to be in the same occupational or industrial area. Census data give little insight into the veracity of these reasons for workers in either capital sector. Further-more, Hoffman (1981) has shown that nonwhites and women receive much less on-the-job training than do white men, even in low-wage jobs.

Instead of treating age only as a characteristic of human capital, new structuralists need to study the relative positions of age groups. Age groups considered cross-sectionally can allow us to look at cohorts of male and female workers who share a common history and present. The relative position of a group at a particular time can be compared with the position of that age group or of that cohort at another time. If we look, for example, at the factors influencing earnings of young workers in 1960, we can see if those factors operate in the same way for young workers in 1980 or for that birth cohort in 1980. Inequalities between age groups in various economic sectors can tell us about the power of workers to attain high rates of return on their characteristics.

The other advantage in comparing age groups lies in the study of women as workers. There is considerable evidence that the earnings determination process operates quite differently for men and women. Human capital theorists cite men's and women's different patterns of labor force participation as the reason for sex differences in earnings. This situation has undoubtedly been more true of older than of younger workers, even in 1980. The separate analysis of the earnings of women and men, and of age groups, allows more valid comparisons and pro-vides some insight into situations women of various ages encounter in the labor market. Data on median annual earnings for age groups of men and women are presented in appendix B, along with other data relevant but not central to my argument.

The Earnings Debate

Although earnings should not be considered the only important out-come of employment, it is the focus in this study. There are several important advantages to studying annual earnings rather than other forms of compensation, such as benefits or hourly wages. First, annual earnings are what most workers have to live on, and their quality of life will be quite dependent on earnings of the household. If home values are not included in net assets, the bottom 90 percent of U.S. households hold only 16.7 percent of all family-owned wealth (*In These Times* 1986). An-nual earnings also provide some indication of the level of nonsalary compensation workers receive (see Freedman 1976). However, earnings have become less representative of the outcomes of labor force participa-tion for workers in all industries, and the differences among industries have increased slightly (wages and salaries constitute a smaller propor-tion of total employee compensation in manufacturing than in non-manufacturing industries [U.S. Department of Labor 1980, pp. 308–18]).

Second, hourly wages will not reflect the true amount of income available to workers because of variations in the number of hours or weeks worked. Hourly wages may be equal for two different jobs, but if one is full-time and the other part-time, their earnings will be quite different. Thus, underemployment is better measured by looking at annual earnings. The importance of considering underemployment as part of the uneven reward structure also dictates that this study include all workers, rather than only those who worked year-round, full-time (at least 35 hours per week and 40 weeks per year). However, results of the same analyses on data from the year-round, full-time (YRFT) labor force are provided in appendix C for interested readers.

Another reason for using annual earnings is data availability. The concern with social change in this study demands comparable data. The 1960 census data do not provide a reliable measure of hourly wage. The earliest data comparable to the 1980 wage data would come from the 1973 Current Population Survey (see Farley 1984). The 1973–80 time period is far less suited to capturing the effects of the changes in class resources discussed in chapter 4 than is the 1960–80 period. Annual earnings can easily be converted to constant dollars by using the Consumer Price Index computed by the Bureau of Labor Statistics to adjust for inflation. The natural logarithm (log) of real earnings is computed to minimize the effect of extremely high earnings.[1]

Finally, the past use of the age-earnings profiles in human capital and some new structuralist studies makes annual earnings a good choice for my study. Age-earnings profiles provide a graphic representation of the median earnings of workers of one age group relative to those of another at each point in time and of the changes between and within sectors across time (using constant dollars). However, age-earnings profiles show only the gross earnings of age groups. Changes in the profiles may reflect more than changes in returns to experience or in the power of seniority. They may also reflect compositional changes—higher levels of education, more women, or occupational shifts. To control for the effects of non-age variables, I used multivariate regression analysis of log earnings.

Regression Analysis of Earnings

There are several ways to evaluate changes in the earnings process. First, the effect of each variable can be considered while statistically controlling for the effects of all others. In this case, regression analysis is conducted on the earnings of all workers in 1960 and 1980. The independent variables included in the regression equation are sex, race (white or nonwhite)[2], age-group membership (the effect of being 25 to 34, 35 to 44, 45 to 54, 55 to 64, or 65 or older relative to the effect of being younger than 25), occupation (having a professional, technical, or managerial occupation compared with being in any other occupation), and economic sector (the effect of employment in core service, core transformative, or periphery service industries relative to the effect of employment in periphery transformative industries).

But the process of earnings determination may vary for men and women, and these differences will be hidden when sex is an independent variable in the regression equation. Looking at the different processes means it is necessary to analyze separately the effects of all of the other independent variables on the earnings of men and of women. Because I am also interested in discovering changes in the position of workers of various ages within economic sectors, and in the differences in the earnings process among economic sectors, I must consider each sector separately. In this case, the independent variables are sex, race, education, occupation, and age group. Again, discovery of the sex-specific processes demands separate analyses for men and women.

Finally, to discover the changes occurring for the age groups, earnings are analyzed separately for each of the six age groups. These analyses enable us to see if the effects of the other independent variables (sex, race, education, occupation, and economic sector) differ among age groups and if the importance of these variables for the earnings of a particular age group (or birth cohort) have changed over time. Again, separate analyses for men and women are required.

The significance of the changes in the regression coefficients of the independent variables is tested with the contrast t statistic.[3] This statistic is also useful for a comparison of the effects of a particular variable in two different groups, for example, the effect of core service employment for men and women.

NOTES

1. Constant dollars are computed by dividing 1979 earnings by the inflation factor since 1959, which is 2.5 (U.S. Department of Labor 1980, p. 185), then aggregating the results into categories corresponding to those used in the 1960 census. The categories used for computation of log earnings are: 50 to 9,950 for $99 intervals from $1 to $9,999; 10,500 to 24,500 for $999 intervals from $10,000 to $24,999; and 25,000 for earnings of $25,000 or more.

2. Treating race as a dichotomous variable presents problems regardless of the dividing lines drawn. Hodson (1978), for example, analyzes earnings of blacks and all others, placing smaller nonblack groups with Caucasians. This approach has the advantage of distinguishing between racial groups on the readily apparent physical characteristic of skin color. The disadvantage lies in placing with whites racial and ethnic groups, such as Hispanics and native Americans, whose labor market experiences are quite distinct from those of whites. Such placement neglects the importance of residential segregation and of physical characteristics other than skin color in employment opportunities and labor market discrimina-

6
The Effects of Economic Change on Earnings

The basic argument presented in previous chapters boils down to this: changes in the what and the how of production will affect the resources available to class actors in their struggle over economic returns. Some of the important structural changes involve worker skill, capital mobility, concentration, and service-sector employment. The tendency overall has been for workers to lose resources formerly available to them. As a class, they are less organized and more fragmented by sex and by workplace. The analyses of earnings in this chapter show a reduction in the rate of return associated with worker characteristics that reflect worker power. Some of these characteristics typically have been considered proxies for human capital—occupation, education, and age. Others reflect structural constraints on employers—the economic sectors. Their diminished importance in the earnings-determination process provides support for a theory of declining working-class resources in the post–World War II era.

CHANGING CHARACTERISTICS OF THE LABOR FORCE

Overall, the labor force was made up of proportionately more women, nonwhites, and young people in 1980 than in 1960. It was more highly educated; nearly twice as many people had some postsecondary education (41.2 percent in 1980, 22.4 percent in 1960), and one and a half times as many were employed in professional, technical, or managerial occupations (see table 6.1).

Table 6.1   Distribution of Labor Force in Economic Sectors by Selected Characteristics, 1960 and 1980 (in percentages)

| | Periphery | | Core | | |
Characteristic	*Transformative*	*Service*	*Transformative*	*Service*	**All Sectors**
Race					
White					
1960	87.9	85.9	92.3	92.9	89.5
1980	80.2	84.8	86.2	85.9	85.2
Nonwhite					
1960	12.1	14.1	7.7	7.1	10.5
1980	19.8	15.2	13.8	14.1	14.8
Sex					
Male					
1960	55.3	45.4	80.0	63.8	61.2
1980	52.2	40.7	74.5	54.4	53.2
Female					
1960	44.7	54.6	20.0	36.2	38.8
1980	47.8	59.3	25.5	45.6	46.8
Occupation					
Professional, Technical, and Managerial					
1960	5.1	23.2	11.9	20.2	17.7
1980	9.3	31.7	17.0	30.5	26.4
Age					
<25					
1960	19.1	24.1	15.4	16.8	19.5
1980	23.5	31.0	21.8	19.8	25.8
25–34					
1960	20.7	19.5	23.9	23.4	21.8
1980	27.0	25.3	28.4	30.9	27.4
35–44					
1960	23.3	20.4	25.6	24.3	23.1
1980	19.3	16.4	19.4	19.9	18.1

The periphery service sector increased its employment share by 6 percent, to 47 percent of nonextractive workers, and core services gained almost 3 percent. The core transformative sector's share of employment declined from one-third of the labor force to about one-fourth. New structuralist literature has generally considered this sector a solid employer. However, Averitt (1968) warned that labor's successes in this sector make labor substitution a likely strategy of employers. The much-touted ability of these manufacturers to control prices and secure their profit margins, an ability that allows them to meet labor's demands for higher wages and improved benefits, also provides the necessary resources to increase productivity through mechanization (Braverman 1974). Finally, note that Averitt's original discussion of the dual economy places multinational corporations (of manufacturing) in the center economy. The rise of the multinational corporate form is apparent in the core transformative sector's sharp loss of employment share (7.1 percent), compared with the much smaller decline in the periphery transformative sector (1.4 percent). The periphery transformative sector also stands out because it employs only a small proportion of the work force (5 percent in 1980). New structuralist reasoning that does not apply to services could clearly not apply to most of the periphery.

Differences among the four sectors in labor force characteristics did not change dramatically between 1960 and 1980, although some tendencies became exaggerated. For example, in periphery services women came to represent nearly 60 percent of workers in 1980, up from 55 percent in 1960. The representation of women in core transformative industries also increased about 5 percent, though only 25 percent of this sector's workers were female in 1980. Although every sector increased employment in professional, technical, and managerial occupations, workers in these occupations came to constitute over 30 percent of the labor force in core and periphery services. Periphery services stood apart from the other sectors in the proportion of workers under age 25; in 1960 24 percent and in 1980 31 percent of periphery service workers were young (compared with 17 percent and 20 percent, respectively, in core services, for examples). Overall, the influx of the baby-boom generation into the work force meant that by 1980 over half of all workers were under age 35.

Comparison of the characteristics of workers in the industrial categories of the core and periphery shows some of the utility in my four-sector approach to economic segmentation. Compared with their transformative industry counterparts, the service sectors of the core and periphery were characterized by more highly educated workers and more females. Racial composition did not differ between the industrial categories of the core in either 1960 or 1980, but over time it did change to more closely reflect the average for the entire labor force. As mentioned above, the transformative and service categories of the capital sectors differed markedly in occupational composition. We would expect that these compositional differences would be reflected in earnings levels for the economic sectors. In 1960 and in 1980 the median earnings (in constant 1959 dollars) were higher in the transformative than in the service industries within the core and the periphery, but the differences between the capital sectors were greater than those within them.

Distribution of Median Annual Earnings by Economic Sectors (in 1959 constant dollars)					
	Periphery		Core		
	Transformative	Service	Transformative	Service	All Sectors
1960	2,400	2,000	4,400	4,200	3,300
1980	3,100	2,400	5,100	4,700	3,600

Let us look more closely at earnings within economic sectors by examining the age-earnings profiles. The profiles allow us to examine the distribution of earnings visually by sector and by age, and they provide a clue to the changing resources available to various groups of workers. First, I present the median earnings for the age groups of men and women in the nonextractive civilian labor force in 1960 and in 1980. Then, I provide separate age-earnings profiles for each economic sector. The combined picture allows us to see the overall differences among the sectors in the earnings-opportunity structure. The separate age-earnings profiles of men and women illustrate the sex-specific nature of opportunities by sector and by age. Since work experience is more likely to be reflected by a man's age than by a woman's, changes in the age-earnings profile of women cannot be used as evidence of declining returns to seniority or experience. Instead, these changes provide an indication of the types of earnings opportunities available to women of various ages.

CHANGES IN THE AGE-EARNINGS PROFILE

Earnings appeared to be distributed by age more unequally in 1980 than in 1960. The age-earnings profiles for all workers (see figure 6.1) were more pitched in shape, and earnings differences between age groups were greater in 1980. For the labor force as a whole, and particularly for men, the age group with the highest median earnings also changed; in 1960, top earners were the 35- to 44-year-olds, but in 1980 45- to 54-year-olds had the highest earnings. This suggests that either the distribution of workers by age into high-paying jobs or industries has changed or that age-related returns have changed within industries. In the first case, we know from the descriptive data (see table 6.1) that the changing age structure of the working population has been reflected fairly evenly in the economic sectors (each has gained or lost approximately the same percentage of workers in any age group). The latter proposition is taken up in the regression analyses that appear in the following sections. However, we can gain insights into the nature of the change in age- and sector-specific earnings by looking at the age-earnings profiles of the economic sectors (see figure 6.2).

Figure 6.1   Age-Earnings Profiles by Sex, 1960 and 1980

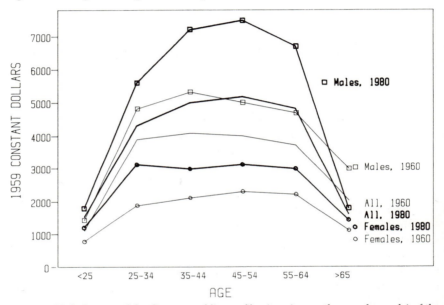

Source: U. S. Bureau of the Census, public use files (one-in-one thousand sample) of the *Censuses of Population and Housing, 1960* and of the *Census of Population and Housing, 1980* (A sample).

The four-sector breakdown of the age-earnings profiles for 1960 and 1980 shows very similar earnings *patterns* between service and transformative industries of the core at each time. However, in 1980 workers between the ages of 35 and 64 in core services earned less than their counterparts in core transformative industries; their earnings had been nearly equal in 1960. The major change appears in the core service sector for groups over age 55—in 1960 their earnings were slightly higher than those of their counterparts in the core transformative sector; in 1980 their earnings were lower. Profiles of earnings in transformative and service industries of the periphery had about the same shapes in 1980 as they had in 1960. Periphery service workers who were younger than 25 or

Figure 6.2   Age-Earnings Profiles by Sector, 1960 and 1980

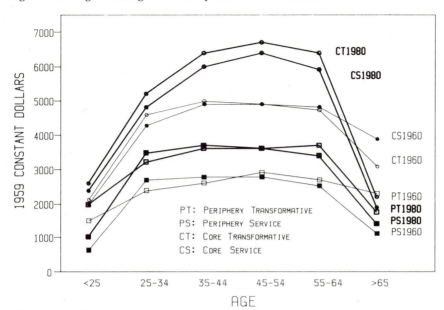

Source: U. S. Bureau of the Census, public use files (one-in-one thousand sample) of the *Censuses of Population and Housing, 1960* and of the *Census of Population and Housing, 1980* (A sample).

older than 54 in 1980 had lower earnings than had their counterparts in the periphery transformative sector (in 1980 the 55- to 64-year-olds were the highest paid cohort in the periphery transformative sector; their counterparts in periphery services earned less than the two next youngest cohorts).

Separating men's from women's earnings in the four sectors makes apparent some of the effects of sex composition of sectors, as well as the remarkable lack of variation in women's earnings. Age-earnings profiles for men are shown in figure 6.3; figure 6.4 shows women's earnings. The age-earnings profiles of women in all sectors are much flatter than men's at both times (note the different scale of earnings). Compared with their counterparts in core transformative industries, men and women in core services had higher earnings levels in both 1960 and 1980, but the gap was largest for middle-aged men (35 to 54) in 1980 and for middle-aged to older women (45 to 64) in 1960. In 1960, women in periphery services had lower earnings than their age-counterparts in every other sector. However, in 1980 earnings in periphery services improved for most age groups of women. This improvement was even more marked for women who worked year-round and full-time (see figure C.4 in appendix C). This appears to be good news for women, since their employment opportunities are concentrated in periphery services industries, such as retail trade and personal services.

Figure 6.3   Age-Earnings Profiles of Males by Sector, 1960 and 1980

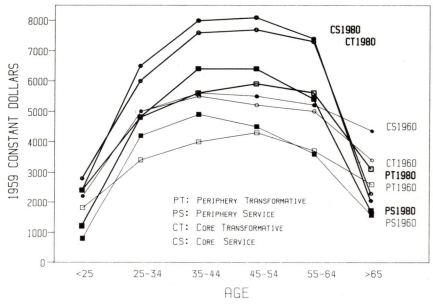

Source: U. S. Bureau of the Census, public use files (one-in-one thousand sample) of the *Censuses of Population and Housing, 1960* and of the *Census of Population and Housing, 1980* (A sample).

In summary, the age-earnings profiles show a change in earnings patterns by age, sector, and sex. Heights of the curves indicate increased inequality between middle-aged workers and those younger and older than they. The decline in the relative position of younger workers (under age 35) is especially apparent for all workers in the core sectors (see figure 6.2) and for men in all sectors, except the periphery transformative industries (see figure 6.3). This finding is consistent with the "baby-boomers' financial bust" argument of Welch (1979), Freeman (1979), and Easterlin, Wachter, and Wachter (1978), which attributes the lower earnings of the post–World War II baby-boom generation to the over-supply of highly educated workers. Experienced and skilled workers benefit from the oversupply of the young, while in unskilled jobs older workers absorb some of the wage losses associated with the entry of the

Figure 6.4   Age-Earnings Profiles of Females by Sector, 1960 and 1980

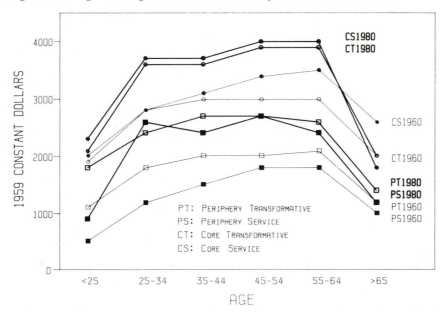

Source: U. S. Bureau of the Census, public use files (one-in-one thousand sample) of the *Censuses of Population and Housing, 1960* and of the *Census of Population and Housing, 1980* (A sample).

large cohorts (Welch 1979). At this point the cohort-size explanation loses credibility. It appears incongruous with the changes in the relative positions of older men in economic sectors. In a sector where many men's jobs are considered skilled—the core service sector—the relative position of 55- to 64-year-olds was lower in 1980 than in 1960, but in the relatively unskilled periphery transformative industries, older men fared better compared with younger workers in 1980 than they had in 1960. The change within the expanding core service sector is especially interesting. Older men in core services in 1960 had median earnings 95 percent of those of men aged 44 to 54; in 1980, their earnings were only 91 percent of the median for men in the 44 to 54 cohort and the real dollar difference increased from $300 to $700 (see tables B.1 and B.2 in appendix B).

Overall, the earnings profiles in core sectors appeared to change the most, though this was especially the case for men. The 1980 median real earnings of all workers in the sectors of the periphery did not even surpass the levels of the core sectors in 1960 (see figure 6.2). Here, however, the predominance of women in periphery services must be held at least partially accountable, since this tendency is not present in the earnings profiles of men. Finally, the sex differences in the earnings of age groups, even within sectors, appeared greater in 1980 than in 1960. The increased sex difference in earnings was found even when only full-time, year-round workers were considered (see table B.2 in appendix B), though Farley (1984) shows that women who can be considered year-round, full-time workers actually work fewer hours per week and fewer weeks per year than male year-round, full-time workers. However, he finds that these differences do not explain the gap in earnings between men and women.

The age-earnings profiles provide an indication that changes since 1960 have influenced the distribution of earnings. To determine the impact of these changes on the earnings-determination process, we need to examine each factor separately while statistically controlling for the effects of other factors. Regression analysis is a valuable tool for this purpose. The following analyses of earnings in 1960 and in 1980 consider the changes for the nonextractive labor force as a whole, for age groups, and for economic sectors. The experience of men and women will be examined separately in each case, since there is ample evidence of significant differences in the ways their characteristics and the characteristics of the economy affect their earnings (Beck, Horan, and Tolbert 1978; Farley 1984; Kalleberg, Wallace, and Althauser 1981).

CHANGES IN THE EARNINGS DETERMINATION PROCESS

In arguing for attention to the changes in the economic structure that affect the resources available to workers and owners, I have focused on the what and the how of production. To capture these dimensions, I modified an existing model of economic segmentation developed by Tolbert, Horan, and Beck (1980) to include the distinctions between transformative and service industries. The age-earnings profiles illustrate some of the usefulness of my model of economic segmentation. Regression analyses of various operationalizations of economic-sector on earnings also support my choice. In table 6.2, I present three models to explain earnings. Model 1 uses the capital sectors of core and periphery developed by Tolbert, Horan, and Beck; model 2 uses two industrial categories—transformative and service—based on distinctions developed by Browning and Singelmann (1978); and model 3 is derived from cross-classification of these capital and industrial sectors. The other independent variables used in each model are sex, race, education, age group, and occupation—professional, technical, or managerial. The contrast t statistic indicates the change between 1960 and 1980 in the effect of each variable on earnings and is reported for all variables in model 3 and for the sector variables in the other models.

Table 6.2   Regression of Log Earnings Models, 1960 and 1980

Variable		Model 1	Model 2	Model 3
Female	1960	−.321 (−.799)	−.345 (−.858)	−.317 (−.788)
	1980	−.252 (−.602)	−.265 (−.634)	−.245 (−.586)
	Contrast t			20.200*
Nonwhite	1960	−.073 (−.287)	−.082 (−.323)	−.069 (−.272)
	1980	−.028 (−.095)	−.031 (−.104)	−.029 (−.096)
	Contrast t			11.131*
Education	1960	.161 (.060)	.186 (.070)	.172 (.064)
	1980	.124 (.051)	.141 (.058)	.133 (.055)
	Contrast t			6.364*
Professional/ managerial	1960	.109 (.347)	.099 (.317)	.114 (.364)
	1980	.131 (.355)	.128 (.347)	.137 (.369)
	Contrast t			.347
Age[a]				
25–34	1960	.316 (.926)	.327 (.959)	.312 (.916)
	1980	.302 (.808)	.315 (.843)	.298 (.798)
	Contrast t			7.867*
35–44	1960	.390 (1.121)	.403 (1.159)	.387 (1.112)
	1980	.322 (.996)	.333 (1.032)	.318 (.985)
	Contrast t			8.130*
45–54	1960	.386 (1.192)	.397 (1.225)	.384 (1.187)
	1980	.322 (1.085)	.334 (1.125)	.320 (1.077)
	Contrast t			6.707*
55–64	1960	.312 (1.161)	.324 (1.203)	.313 (1.163)
	1980	.271 (1.039)	.279 (1.072)	.269 (1.033)
	Contrast t			6.989*
65 +	1960	.107 (.641)	.112 (.670)	.109 (.652)
	1980	.033 (.226)	.036 (.242)	.034 (.233)
	Contrast t			15.149*
Sector				
Core	1960	.207 (.503)	-- --	-- --
	1980	.198 (.472)	-- --	-- --
	Contrast t	3.100*		
Service	1960	-- --	−.141 (−.348)	-- --
	1980	-- --	−.135 (−.346)	-- --
	Contrast t		.175	
Periphery service[b]	1960	-- --	-- --	−.162 (−.400)
	1980	-- --	-- --	−.143 (−.341)
	Contrast t			2.602*

Table 6.2 (continued)

Variable			Model 1		Model 2		Model 3	
Core	1960		--	--	--	--	.067	(.170)
transformative[b]	1980		--	--	--	--	.074	(.200)
	Contrast t						1.323	
Core service[b]	1960		--	--	--	--	.049	(.153)
	1980		--	--	--	--	.046	(.134)
	Contrast t						.811	
Core sector	1960		--	--	--	--	.687	
contrast[c]	1980		--	--	--	--	3.111*	
Intercept	1960		5.743		6.621		6.540	
	1980		6.099		6.938		6.823	
Adjusted R^2	1960		.399		.378		.405	
	1980		.343		.323		.347	

Source: U. S. Bureau of the Census, public use files (one-in-one thousand sample) of the *Censuses of Population and Housing, 1960* and of the *Census of Population and Housing, 1980* (A sample).

Note: Data are for private-sector workers in nonextractive industries with annual earnings greater than $0 (1959 constant dollars). The standardized coefficients appear without parentheses and are all significant at the .05 level. The metric coefficients are in parentheses. The contrast t is the t statistic of the differences in the metric coefficients in 1960 and 1980. In 1960, N = 58,054; in 1980, N = 99,338.

[a]The excluded age group for 1960 is 14–24; for 1980, 16–24.

[b]Relative to the periphery transformative sector.

[c]T statistic for differences between transformative and service sectors of the core.

*Significance at the .05 level.

Assessing Overall Changes

The amount of variance in earnings (adjusted R^2) explained by the three models does not differ much in either 1960 or 1980, and all models do a better job of accounting for earnings differences in 1960 than they do in 1980. (I will return to this reduction in explanatory power later in this chapter.) Focusing on the differences between the models, several points deserve elaboration. First, model 2, which uses industrial category for sector differentiation, is the least effective of the three models. Working in transformative industries does not contribute as much to individuals' earnings as does working in core-sector industries (compare coefficients for sector in models 1 and 2). Second, there are differences between the models in the changing importance of the sectors. The effect of core-sector employment declined significantly in model 1 between 1960 and 1980 (contrast t statistic for sector), but neither of the core sectors in model 3 had significant changes. However, the penalty associated with periphery service employment was reduced. Furthermore, changes in the metric (unstandardized) regression coefficients for the core transformative and core service sectors are in opposite directions, increasing in the former and decreasing in the latter. These changes suggest that the decline in the importance of core-sector employment, shown in model 1, is a reflection of the improvements in periphery service employment and of the changing industrial composition of the core—away from transformative employment.

Finally, although the effects of employment in the core transformative and core service industries, net of other characteristics, did not change, the differences between being employed in transformative or service industries within the core did. In 1960, there was no significant difference between the economic returns associated with the core sectors; by 1980, the returns for core service employment were significantly less than the returns for core transformative employment (t statistic for core-sector contrast). These changes within the core also occurred for men (see table 6.3). For women, core service employment was significantly less beneficial than core transformative employment in both 1960 and 1980. These contrasts provide further support for my four-sector approach to economic segmentation. The type of industrial employment is important, even when organizational differences have been taken into account.

Table 6.3   Regression of Log Earnings Model for Men and Women, 1960 and 1980

Variable		Men	Women	Sex Contrast
Nonwhite	1960	−.095 (−.328)	−.036 (−.140)	6.643*
	1980	−.076 (−.242)	.017 (.055)	17.441*
	Contrast t	4.623*	7.144*	
Education	1960	.189 (.056)	.187 (.079)	7.273*
	1980	.144 (.051)	.133 (.058)	3.131*
	Contrast t	3.536*	5.824*	
Professional/	1960	.117 (.304)	.136 (.473)	6.298*
managerial	1980	.110 (.275)	.174 (.463)	11.463*
	Contrast t	1.857*	.366	
Age[a]				
25–34	1960	.498 (1.195)	.178 (.560)	23.583*
	1980	.399 (.990)	.233 (.605)	22.608*
	Contrast t	11.514*	1.703*	
35–44	1960	.582 (1.391)	.261 (.779)	23.469*
	1980	.446 (1.281)	.227 (.683)	31.131*
	Contrast t	5.966*	3.605*	

Table 6.3 (continued)

Variable			Men	Women	Sex Contrast
45–54	1960		.541 (1.400)	.304 (.965)	16.156*
	1980		.429 (1.329)	.249 (.824)	24.496*
	Contrast t		3.716*	5.033*	
55–64	1960		.432 (1.322)	.262 (1.028)	9.368*
	1980		.351 (1.231)	.221 (.840)	17.146*
	Contrast t		4.280*	5.794*	
65 +	1960		.161 (.776)	.089 (.589)	3.905*
	1980		.044 (.273)	.033 (.218)	1.486
	Contrast t		15.464*	7.269*	
Sector[b]					
Periphery service	1960		−.104 (−.229)	−.245 (−.619)	11.249*
	1980		−.112 (−.258)	−.177 (−.417)	5.470*
	Contrast t		1.079	5.549*	
Core	1960		.093 (.190)	.060 (.198)	.215
transformative	1980		.091 (.208)	.057 (.188)	.649
	Contrast t		.688	.246	
Core service	1960		.068 (.174)	.025 (.084)	2.332*
	1980		.052 (.141)	.037 (.105)	1.176
	Contrast t		1.196	.511	
Core sector	1960		.580	2.480*	--
contrast[c]	1980		2.560*	2.395*	--
Intercept	1960		6.382	5.891	--
	1980		6.709	6.360	--
Adjusted R^2	1960		.387	.222	--
	1980		.368	.201	--
N	1960		35,507	22,547	--
	1980		52,885	46,453	--

Source: U. S. Bureau of the Census, public use files (one-in-one thousand sample) of the *Censuses of Population and Housing, 1960* and of the *Census of Population and Housing, 1980* (A sample).

Note: Data are for private-sector workers in nonextractive industries with annual earnings greater than $0 (1959 constant dollars). The standardized coefficients appear without parentheses and are all significant at the .05 level. The metric coefficients are in parentheses. The contrast t is the t statistic of the differences in the metric coefficients in 1960 and 1980. The asterisk indicates significance at the .05 level.

[a]The excluded age group for 1960 is 14–24; for 1980, 16–24.

[b]Relative to the periphery transformative sector.

[c]T statistic for differences between transformative and service sectors of the core.

*Significance at the .05 level.

The remainder of my discussion about the changes in the earnings determination process for all workers focuses on model 3. I briefly discuss the changes in the effects of each independent variable and then examine the differences between men and women.

In the full regression model, the effects of sex and race were significantly reduced between 1960 and 1980. If we consider these effects a loose (and highly imperfect) measure of discrimination, it is apparent that labor market discrimination against nonwhites and women has been reduced. This conclusion, of course, assumes that women and nonwhites have the same educational and employment opportunities as white men. It cannot account for the institutionalized discrimination that restricts the opportunities of women and nonwhites by indirectly restricting their educational or employment choices. That educational attainment was less important to earnings in 1980 than in 1960 suggests that education is not valued so much at it was in the past. Looking at the same time period, but considering elementary and secondary education separate from college education, Farley (1984) found increased rates of return for elementary and secondary education and decreased rates of return for college education (also see Freedman 1976).[1] Those in the labor market seem to be finding that the expectations for educational attainment are going up but the rewards are going down (see Bowles and Gintis 1976; Collins 1979).

The standardized regression coefficients show that for all workers in 1980 it was relatively more important to be in a professional, technical, or managerial occupation than to have additional years of schooling. College graduates of the mid-1970s and beyond recognize this as part of the reward structure associated with being in the right area at the right time. They know that it is not just the college degree that is important; it is the major field of study. The greater importance of occupation over schooling in 1980 appeared to be particularly the case for women (see table 6.3).

Relative to workers less than 25 years old, every age group in the labor force as a whole received lower rates of return in 1980 than it had in 1960. This was also true for men and for women (except those 25 to 34 years old). In 1960 and 1980, the coefficients for each age group are extremely different for men and women (reflected by the t statistic in the column "Sex Contrast" in table 6.3). In fact, age-related returns became more dissimilar for the sexes over the 20 years. The diminished returns to age provide support for the argument that changes in the economy have reduced the ability of workers to advance their earnings by advancing in age.

As I discussed above, there also have been changes in the advantages and disadvantages of being employed in a particular economic sector. The biggest change is a reduction of the earnings disadvantage of periphery service employment. The separate analyses for men and women reveal that this is occurring only for women. However, given that 60 percent of women employed in 1980 worked in periphery service industries, this change is important.

Finally, let us look at the overall effectiveness of the model in explaining the variation in earnings. The model accounts for less variance in 1980 than it had in 1960; this was true for the whole labor force and for each sex. Featherman and Hauser (1978) reported similar results in their sectoral analysis of men's earnings in 1962 and in 1973. They conclude that segmentation is becoming less important, a conclusion supported by the changes in the effects of core sector employment in my analysis (model 1, table 6.2). However, the lack of significant change in the effects of the economic sectors in my model on men's earnings does not support their conclusion. In fact, it appears that individual characteristics, typically considered human capital, are becoming less important to earnings.

It is no surprise that the model does a much better job of explaining men's earnings than women's. Hodson (1983) reports only marginal significance of his industry-level model for women's earnings. The differences between the earnings determination processes for men and women are further highlighted by the tests of differences in the effects of each variable (see table 6.3). The only variables that did not have significantly different rates of return for the sexes were core transformative employment in both years and core service employment in 1980. These differences support the claims by new structuralists that separate forces operate for men and women in the labor market.

Changes within Economic Sectors

Applying regression analysis to the earnings of workers within each economic sector allows us to see how the effects of each of the human capital and demographic variables have changed for workers in different employment contexts and provides an indication of the changes in the work setting. Changes within the sectors and comparisons of the core transformative and core service sectors are important indicators of the changing resources of class actors—workers and employers. Table 6.4 provides the results of the analyses of workers' earnings in 1960 and in 1980 by economic sector. Results of similar analyses for men and for women appear in tables 6.5 and 6.6. The returns associated with age are especially interesting because they provide an indication of the power that accompanies age in each sector.

Age and change. Relative to workers less than 25 years old, all other age groups in periphery service and core transformative industries received a lower rate of return for their labor force participation in 1980 than in

1960 (table 6.4). However, the rate of return for all but the oldest age group improved in the core service sector. These improvements were not large enough to eliminate the differences between the core transformative and core service sectors in the rates of return to age groups, except for workers 25 to 34 years old (see table B.3 in appendix B).

The changes in age-related returns in the sectors provide support for my argument that, net of other characteristics, age is granting fewer protections and privileges to workers than it did in the past. Although I did not expect this finding in periphery services, in retrospect it should not really be a surprise. After raising their children, women could more easily enter this sector than other sectors, and many such women did enter the labor force in the 1970s. Freeman (1979, p. 291) suggests that "the intermittent work experience of women makes younger women and older women closer substitutes in production." The separate analyses for the sexes reveal, however, that men in periphery services experienced reductions in returns to age similar to those of women (compare tables 6.5 and 6.6).

The decline in the returns associated with age in core transformative industries is consistent with my expectations, given the changes that have occurred in manufacturing—declines in unionization and seniority provisions, increased price competition within industries, international and regional mobility of capital, and deskilling. These are changes that weaken the ability of this sector's more powerful workers (middle-aged and older men) to protect their earnings from economic stagnation and decline. The analyses for the sexes support this power interpretation; the declines show up for men in this sector, but not for most age groups of women.

The positive changes for age groups in core service industries stand in marked contrast to the decline in core transformative industries, suggesting several things. First, core services provided better employment opportunities (at least in terms of pay) in 1980 than they did in the past. The differences in the returns to age between the two core sectors diminished, though they remained significantly lower in services for most age groups. Second, the increased returns to age, net of other characteristics, suggest that core services may be becoming increasingly hierarchical and bureaucratic in their control of workers. Bluestone and his colleagues (1981) take the increasingly peaked age-earnings profiles of men in the department-store industry as an indicator of this trend. The sex-specific analysis in my study also supports their interpretation. The increased rate of return shows up for middle-aged men (35 to 54 years old) and for women 25 to 44 years old. Younger men and older men and women did not significantly benefit from the changes in core services.

Other changes within sectors. The picture emerging from the analysis of earnings for the whole labor force (table 6.4) shows improvement for

Table 6.4 Regression of Log Earnings Model by Economic Sector, 1960 and 1980

Variable		Periphery		Core	
		Transformative	Service	Transformative	Service
Female	1960	-.313 (-.635)	-.345 (-.933)	-.276 (-.659)	-.358 (-.744)
	1980	-.246 (-.522)	-.240 (-.615)	-.248 (-.573)	-.279 (-.585)
	Contrast t	2.800*	18.483*	4.664*	7.350*
Nonwhite	1960	-.082 (-.254)	-.059 (-.227)	-.094 (-.339)	-.058 (-.224)
	1980	-.047 (-.126)	[-.007] (-.023)	-.071 (-.207)	-.048 (-.143)
	Contrast t	2.269*	7.884*	5.115*	2.206*
Education	1960	.169 (.055)	.174 (.069)	.207 (.064)	.135 (.047)
	1980	.150 (.053)	.130 (.054)	.146 (.054)	.127 (.051)
	Contrast t	.283	4.160*	3.536*	.943
Professional/ managerial	1960	.124 (.570)	.138 (.444)	.105 (.310)	.088 (.220)
	1980	.137 (.498)	.175 (.473)	.102 (.275)	.095 (.214)
	Contrast t	.857	1.243	1.409	.230
Age[a]					
25–34	1960	.247 (.615)	.313 (1.062)	.400 (.896)	.260 (.612)
	1980	.237 (.567)	.296 (.856)	.332 (.743)	.316 (.713)
	Contrast t	.813	8.341*	6.530*	3.194*
35–44	1960	.338 (.806)	.385 (1.287)	.498 (1.091)	.333 (.774)
	1980	.286 (.770)	.303 (1.028)	.373 (.951)	.347 (.906)
	Contrast t	.557	10.036*	5.813*	4.099*

45–54	1960	.359 (.905)	.400 (1.394)	.469 (1.120)	.329 (.847)
	1980	.272 (.804)	.309 (1.148)	.380 (1.035)	.338 (.968)
	Contrast t	1.474	10.036*	3.334*	3.457*
55–64	1960	.294 (.905)	.332 (1.364)	.372 (1.109)	.268 (.806)
	1980	.261 (.860)	.270 (1.121)	.310 (.968)	.265 (.893)
	Contrast t	.581	7.888*	4.726*	2.254*
65+	1960	.093 (.461)	.136 (.817)	.099 (.546)	.080 (.398)
	1980	[.025] (.149)	.059 (.382)	[.001] (.010)	[-.002] (-.012)
	Contrast t	2.775*	10.163*	10.240*	6.401*
Intercept	1960	6.776	6.005	6.736	7.175
	1980	6.973	6.414	7.105	7.148
Adjusted R²	1960	.250	.365	.325	.287
	1980	.223	.300	.285	.286
N	1960	3,729	23,729	19,751	10,845
	1980	5,002	46,669	26,511	21,156

Source: U. S. Bureau of the Census, public use files (one-in-one thousand sample) of the *Censuses of Population and Housing, 1960* and of the *Census of Population and Housing, 1980* (A sample).

Note: Data are for private-sector workers in nonextractive industries with annual earnings greater than $0 (1959 constant dollars). The standardized coefficients appear without parentheses and are all significant at the .05 level unless enclosed in square brackets. The metric coefficients are in parentheses. The contrast t is the t statistic of the differences in the metric coefficients in 1960 and 1980.

[a]The excluded age group for 1960 is 14–24; for 1980, 16–24.

*Significance at the .05 level.

Table 6.5 Regression of Log Earnings Model for Men within Economic Sectors, 1960 and 1980

Variable		Periphery		Core	
		Transformative	Service	Transformative	Service
Nonwhite	1960	-.151 (-.414)	-.083 (-.315)	-.106 (-.342)	-.100 (-.288)
	1980	-.078 (-.221)	[-.057] (-.201)	-.098 (-.275)	-.100 (-.285)
	Contrast t	2.647*	3.236*	2.410*	.081
Education	1960	.223 (.065)	.165 (.056)	.226 (.061)	.165 (.040)
	1980	.209 (.071)	.106 (.040)	.172 (.057)	.154 (.049)
	Contrast t	.707	3.771*	1.414	2.121*
Professional/ managerial	1960	.141 (.515)	.105 (.294)	.122 (.312)	.133 (.242)
	1980	.129 (.400)	.138 (.363)	.094 (.229)	.081 (.164)
	Contrast t	1.242	2.240*	3.256*	2.972*
Age[a]					
25–34	1960	.321 (.787)	.497 (1.462)	.515 (1.060)	.548 (.995)
	1980	.304 (.730)	.404 (1.153)	.378 (.798)	.471 (.991)
	Contrast t	.731	4.231*	10.277*	.106
35–44	1960	.418 (.980)	.557 (1.700)	.615 (1.246)	.659 (1.176)
	1980	.349 (.960)	.431 (1.488)	.441 (1.061)	.547 (1.299)
	Contrast t	.244	5.851*	7.068*	3.212*

		Model 1	Model 2	Model 3	Model 4
45–54	1960	.413 (1.027)	.515 (1.671)	.577 (1.265)	.600 (1.183)
	1980	.359 (1.091)	.396 (1.521)	.477 (1.135)	.519 (1.314)
	Contrast t	.748	3.985*	4.713*	3.300*
55–64	1960	.337 (.975)	.402 (1.511)	.459 (1.229)	.496 (1.116)
	1980	.324 (1.089)	.332 (1.401)	.363 (1.054)	.402 (1.179)
	Contrast t	1.194	2.618*	5.619*	1.434
65+	1960	.133 (.539)	.171 (.884)	.135 (.654)	.202 (.714)
	1980	.082 (.481)	.078 (.479)	[−.007] (−.049)	.028 (.147)
	Contrast t	.417	7.139*	12.859*	9.009*
Intercept	1960	6.607	5.969	6.632	6.932
	1980	6.638	6.443	7.018	6.930
Adjusted R²	1960	.274	.406	.326	.286
	1980	.239	.378	.285	.310
N	1960	2,046	10,760	15,790	6,911
	1980	2,609	19,011	19,760	11,505

Source: U. S. Bureau of the Census, public use files (one-in-one thousand sample) of the *Censuses of Population and Housing, 1960* and of the *Census of Population and Housing, 1980* (A sample).

Note: Data are for private-sector workers in nonextractive industries with annual earnings greater than $0 (1959 constant dollars). The stand-ardized coefficients appear without parentheses and are all significant at the .05 level unless enclosed in square brackets. The metric coefficients are in parentheses. The contrast t is the t statistic of the differences in the metric coefficients in 1960 and 1980.

[a]The excluded age group for 1960 is 14–24; for 1980, 16–24.

*Significance at the .05 level.

Table 6.6 Regression of Log Earnings Model for Women within Economic Sectors, 1960 and 1980

		Periphery		Core	
Variable		Transformative	Service	Transformative	Service
Nonwhite	1960	[.025] (.084)	-.037 (-.133)	-.081 (-.358)	[-.015] (-.072)
	1980	[-.025] (-.058)	.028 (.094)	[-.011] (-.033)	[.004] (.012)
	Contrast t	9.823*	6.651*	4.352*	1.054
Education	1960	.088 (.031)	.203 (.083)	.176 (.073)	.136 (.074)
	1980	.078 (.027)	.148 (.064)	.091 (.040)	.094 (.046)
	Contrast t	.351	3.800*	3.579*	2.720*
Professional/ managerial	1960	.084 (.593)	.165 (.528)	.055 (.284)	.043 (.148)
	1980	.123 (.562)	.199 (.521)	.123 (.389)	.120 (.277)
	Contrast t	.161	.203	1.192	2.150*
Age[a]					
25–34	1960	.170 (.391)	.210 (.719)	.165 (.403)	.099 (.264)
	1980	.169 (.367)	.233 (.647)	.263 (.595)	.235 (.505)
	Contrast t	.269	1.961*	3.343*	4.345*
35–44	1960	.266 (.583)	.301 (.967)	.282 (.649)	.145 (.386)
	1980	.224 (.538)	.228 (.732)	.252 (.651)	.213 (.545)
	Contrast t	.496	6.370*	.034	2.767*

		(1)		(2)		(3)		(4)	
45–54	1960	.313	(.722)	.356	(1.176)	.271	(.704)	.203	(.602)
	1980	.186	(.488)	.261	(.909)	.267	(.758)	.222	(.649)
	Contrast t	2.427*		6.976*		.841		.743	
55–64	1960	.261	(.780)	.312	(1.233)	.222	(.797)	.171	(.621)
	1980	.200	(.587)	.236	(.925)	.221	(.735)	.188	(.665)
	Contrast t	1.738*		6.984*		.798		.591	
65+	1960	.061	(.405)	.128	(.782)	.043	(.331)	[.024]	(.169)
	1980	-.045	(-.245)	.048	(.309)	.027	(.194)	[-.002]	(-.012)
	Contrast t	3.241*		7.034*		.921		1.389	
Intercept	1960	6.502		5.072		6.324		6.333	
	1980	6.903		5.798		6.821		6.782	
Adjusted R²	1960	.079		.222		.091		.057	
	1980	.079		.199		.107		.105	
N	1960	1,683		12,969		3,961		3,934	
	1980	2,393		27,658		6,751		9,651	

Source: U. S. Bureau of the Census, public use files (one-in-one thousand sample) of the *Censuses of Population and Housing, 1960* and of the *Census of Population and Housing, 1980* (A sample).

Note: Data are for private-sector workers in nonextractive industries with annual earnings greater than $0 (1959 constant dollars). The standardized coefficients appear without parentheses and are all significant at the .05 level unless enclosed in square brackets. The metric coefficients are in parentheses. The contrast t is the t statistic of the differences in the metric coefficients in 1960 and 1980.

ᵃThe excluded age group for 1960 is 14–24; for 1980, 16–24.

*Significance at the .05 level.

women and nonwhites in every sector, but particularly where women are heavily concentrated, in periphery service industries. In this sector, the rate of return to education diminished between 1960 and 1980, and additional schooling became less important than having a professional or managerial position. In the other sectors, educational advancements remained relatively more important than occupation. The changes in periphery services suggest that lower-level occupations are now being filled by persons with higher education levels than in the past. This interpretation is also supported by the reduction in returns to education for women in all sectors except the periphery transformative sector (see table 6.6). Furthermore, in 1980, having a professional or managerial occupation was relatively more important than educational advancement to women's earnings in every sector.

The lack of significant change in the returns to occupation for the labor force in any sector indicates that within economic sectors there has not been an increased divergence of earnings by occupation. Stanback and Noyelle (1982) argue that the growth of services (occupations as well as industries) contributes to an economic division of jobs, between good and bad ones. The good jobs are the professional, technical, and managerial ones; the bad jobs are most other types of occupations. According to Stanback and Noyelle, even transformative industries in the core are affected by this occupational bifurcation. However, my sectoral analysis of earnings shows that having a professional or managerial occupation contributes more to earnings in the periphery sectors than it does in core sectors. Within the core, the occupation variable had more effect on earnings of workers in transformative industries than it did in service industries in 1980, but this was also true in 1960. Only the growth of periphery services would seem to be contributing to an economic bifurcation of work. The increased importance of occupation for men in that sector and its decreased importance for men in the core sectors further support this argument.

Core services have one other distinctive feature that I have not yet discussed. For men in this sector, the effects of being nonwhite on earnings did not change significantly between 1960 and 1980. This is especially striking given the reductions in the effects of race for men in the other sectors. Other studies have also suggested that development of the service economy will not benefit blacks (Stanback and Noyelle 1982; see also Business Week 1986). Perhaps the professional and social components of work in this sector (such as contact with clients) are being used to justify keeping nonwhites in the lower-paying, lower-status positions. This would be especially likely for nonwhite males; white females are as likely as their nonwhite counterparts to be relegated to low-paying positions (the effect of race for females in core services was not significant in either 1960 or 1980).

Changes within Age Groups

In my discussion of age as a correlate of power, I suggest that the position of age groups relative to each other may be changing and that particular sectors provide fewer advantages or protections to vulnerable age groups. In the previous section I dealt with the changes in the relative positions of age groups within economic sectors; in this section I concentrate on changes in the returns to personal and employment characteristics for workers of common ages.

Individuals' characteristics. Several trends appear in the earnings process for most age groups of workers (table 6.7). As expected, the negative effect of being female is reduced across the board. The effect of race is also significantly smaller for every age group except workers less than 25 years old; for that group being nonwhite was a greater detriment to annual earnings in 1980 than it had been in 1960. This negative effect is also found in the separate analyses for men and women (see tables 6.8 and 6.9). Observers of the high unemployment rate of black youths will not be shocked by this finding, since these young people are also more likely to be underemployed if they do manage to find work. That the earnings penalty for nonwhite youth has increased should, nonetheless, be quite disturbing.

Another common trend is the reduction in returns to education for all but the oldest group of workers. Nearly all women's age groups share in this trend, though only younger groups of men (those under age 35) in 1980 experienced lower rates of return to education than did their age counterparts in 1960. Comparing the education and occupation effects (especially the standardized coefficients) for age groups helps us understand how the reward structure for workers has changed. In 1960, education was more important than professional or managerial occupation to workers in every group under age 65. In 1980, that was still true for workers in the older half of the age distribution, but for the younger half, having a professional or managerial position was relatively more important than investing in additional years of education. For workers between the ages of 25 and 44, the returns to occupation were significantly increased, while workers 45 to 54 years old had lower returns.

Sectoral changes. Compared with employment in the periphery transformative sector, employment in periphery services became less detrimental to the earnings of young workers (less than 25 years old), although its effect remained strongly negative in 1980. Young workers also gained less from employment in core services in 1980 than did young workers in 1960. In fact, for young workers in 1980, core service employment did not bring significantly higher earnings than did employment in periphery transformative industries. The overall effect of these changes was to make the core transformative sector the best earnings

Table 6.7 Regression of Log Earnings Model by Age Group, 1960 and 1980

Variable		<25		25–34		35–44		45–54		55–64		65+	
Female	1960	−.141	(−.378)	−.453	(−1.020)	−.467	(−1.010)	−.423	(−.870)	−.356	(−.741)	−.244	(−.652)
	1980	−.108	(−.261)	−.311	(−.629)	−.407	(−.859)	−.389	(−.789)	−.334	(−.692)	−.156	(−.406)
	Contrast t	4.211*		19.310*		7.359*		3.693*		1.724*		3.582*	
Nonwhite	1960	[−.011]	(−.053)	−.092	(−.302)	−.088	(−.289)	−.110	(−.369)	−.111	(−.390)	−.050	(−.227)
	1980	−.052	(−.177)	−.031	(−.083)	−.019	(−.056)	−.024	(−.072)	−.039	(−.127)	[.026]	(.108)
	Contrast t	2.773*		7.882*		7.978*		8.886*		5.868*		3.049*	
Education	1960	.156	(.094)	.149	(.052)	.189	(.063)	.222	(.066)	.216	(.060)	.152	(.049)
	1980	.108	(.065)	.121	(.044)	.157	(.054)	.183	(.057)	.170	(.053)	.140	(.050)
	Contrast t	4.022*		2.219*		2.496*		2.496*		1.650*		.101	
Professional/ managerial	1960	.091	(.411)	.085	(.225)	.119	(.315)	.157	(.406)	.157	(.416)	.185	(.599)
	1980	.114	(.394)	.156	(.335)	.162	(.363)	.161	(.354)	.161	(.379)	.118	(.367)
	Contrast t	.369		4.218*		1.874*		1.870*		1.016		2.707*	
Sector[a]													
Periphery service	1960	−.312	(−.834)	−.106	(−.236)	−.117	(−.255)	−.141	(−.290)	−.159	(−.325)	−.177	(−.447)
	1980	−.254	(−.616)	−.103	(−.209)	−.116	(−.247)	−.091	(−.185)	−.140	(−.291)	−.135	(−.355)
	Contrast t	3.655*		.631		.189		2.320*		.561		.664	

	(1)	(2)	(3)	(4)	(5)	(6)
Core transformative 1960	[.019] (.058)	.094 (.208)	.091 (.197)	.071 (.148)	.084 (.180)	[.028] (.080)
1980	.047 (.136)	.111 (.251)	.081 (.189)	.112 (.248)	.067 (.151)	[-.007] (-.022)
Contrast t	1.176	.990	.185	2.080*	.500	.689
Core service 1960	.035 (.127)	.071 (.190)	.048 (.126)	.041 (.107)	.044 (.112)	[.047] (.151)
1980	[.005] (.017)	.092 (.218)	.065 (.163)	.076 (.182)	[.025] (.062)	[-.021] (-.069)
Contrast t	1.659*	.622	.830	1.560	.821	1.467
Intercept 1960	6.237	7.628	7.707	7.715	7.701	7.275
1980	6.734	7.706	7.898	7.872	7.933	7.093
Adjusted R² 1960	.178	.354	.403	.391	.339	.218
1980	.129	.217	.325	.328	.274	.090
N 1960	11,317	12,708	13,451	11,056	7,033	2,489
1980	25,616	27,231	17,981	14,591	10,751	3,168

Source: U. S. Bureau of the Census, public use files (one-in-one thousand sample) of the *Censuses of Population and Housing, 1960* and of the *Census of Population and Housing, 1980* (A sample).

Note: Data are for private-sector workers in nonextractive industries with annual earnings greater than $0 (1959 constant dollars). The standardized coefficients appear without parentheses and are all significant at the .05 level unless enclosed in square brackets. The metric coefficients are in parentheses. The contrast t is the t statistic of the differences in the metric coefficients in 1960 and 1980.

[a]Excluded category is periphery transformative sector.

*Significance at the .05 level.

Table 6.8 Regression of Log Earnings Model for Men within Age Group, 1960 and 1980

Variable		<25	25–34	35–44	45–54	55–64	65+
Nonwhite	1960	[-.015] (-.067)	-.210 (-.477)	-.160 (-.349)	-.144 (-.361)	-.125 (-.366)	[-.038] (-.166)
	1980	-.068 (-.230)	-.140 (-.308)	-.119 (-.260)	-.109 (-.262)	-.062 (-.183)	[.064] (.284)
	Contrast t	2.641*	5.909*	2.997*	2.637*	3.401*	3.059*
Education	1960	.150 (.080)	.200 (.042)	.324 (.064)	.282 (.060)	.216 (.049)	.139 (.042)
	1980	.093 (.054)	.117 (.033)	.256 (.059)	.263 (.059)	.209 (.052)	.162 (.055)
	Contrast t	3.022*	2.121*	1.387	.235	.707	1.080
Professional/ managerial	1960	.083 (.359)	.090 (.148)	.147 (.235)	.194 (.358)	.198 (.424)	.219 (.663)
	1980	.087 (.310)	.126 (.219)	.148 (.241)	.151 (.253)	.178 (.341)	.158 (.478)
	Contrast t	.776	2.772*	.242	3.532*	2.013*	1.710*
Sector[a]							
Periphery service	1960	-.283 (-.734)	[.007] (.010)	[-.006] (-.009)	-.063 (-.103)	-.102 (-.182)	-.159 (-.389)
	1980	-.235 (-.565)	-.053 (-.091)	[-.020] (-.034)	-.067 (-.117)	-.123 (-.232)	-.210 (-.556)
	Contrast t	2.086*	2.160*	.542	.260	.714	.936

	Model 1	Model 2	Model 3	Model 4	Model 5	Model 6
Core transformative 1960	[.005] (.014)	.207 (.288)	.197 (.259)	.153 (.222)	.157 (.255)	[.046] (.116)
1980	.077 (.198)	.159 (.264)	.178 (.281)	.148 (.236)	.092 (.162)	[-.108] (-.336)
Contrast t	2.232*	.538	.499	.271	1.370	2.448*
Core service 1960	[.006] (.023)	.164 (.281)	.143 (.229)	.106 (.192)	.110 (.216)	[.081] (.233)
1980	[-.004] (-.014)	.142 (.269)	.164 (.292)	.108 (.196)	[.033] (.067)	[-.115] (-.360)
Contrast t	.399	.249	1.367	.073	2.086*	3.137*
Intercept 1960	6.388	7.656	7.603	7.687	7.702	7.268
1980	6.851	7.877	7.770	7.889	7.939	7.230
Adjusted R² 1960	.115	.164	.252	.239	.202	.146
1980	.106	.103	.175	.177	.142	.074
N 1960	6,056	8,264	8,347	6,734	4,450	1,656
1980	12,951	14,614	9,640	7,999	5,693	1,718

Source: U. S. Bureau of the Census, public use files (one-in-one thousand sample) of the *Censuses of Population and Housing, 1960* and of the *Census of Population and Housing, 1980* (A sample).

Note: Data are for private-sector workers in nonextractive industries with annual earnings greater than $0 (1959 constant dollars). The standardized coefficients appear without parentheses and are all significant at the .05 level unless enclosed in square brackets. The metric coefficients are in parentheses. The contrast t is the t statistic of the differences in the metric coefficients in 1960 and 1980.

[a]Excluded category is periphery transformative sector.

*Significance at the .05 level.

Table 6.9 Regression of Log Earnings Model for Women within Age Group, 1960 and 1980

Variable		<25		25–34		35–44		45–54		55–64		65+
Nonwhite	1960	[−.004]	−.018	[−.000]	(−.001)	−.047	(−.158)	−.100	(−.340)	−.109	(−.388)	−.074	(−.312)
	1980	−.036	−.123	.051	(.140)	.048	(.138)	.042	(.121)	[−.021]	[−.066]	[−.013]	(−.047)
	Contrast t	2.189*		2.562*		5.390*		7.730*		4.088*		1.541	
Education	1960	.169	(.116)	.161	(.075)	.149	(.061)	.236	(.078)	.273	(.081)	.202	(.069)
	1980	.128	(.079)	.147	(.061)	.118	(.047)	.157	(.055)	.163	(.005)	.109	(.040)
	Contrast t	3.421*		1.565		1.793*		2.945*		3.329*		1.768*	
Professional/ managerial	1960	.113	(.515)	.134	(.443)	.152	(.485)	.176	(.495)	.139	(.387)	.142	(.455)
	1980	.142	(.470)	.199	(.453)	.214	(.500)	.210	(.477)	.176	(.432)	.075	(.232)
	Contrast t	.649		.441		.270		.328		.646		1.542	
Sector[a] Periphery service	1960	−.344	(−.942)	−.234	(−.576)	−.220	(−.513)	−.223	(−.489)	−.229	(−.510)	−.220	(−.628)
	1980	−.276	(−.680)	−.152	(−.329)	−.199	(−.429)	−.123	(−.251)	−.166	(−.350)	[−.037]	(−.097)
	Contrast t	2.961*		3.174*		1.097		3.114*		1.666*		2.158*	

Core transformative 1960	[.051] (.190)	.071 (.216)	.089 (.255)	.047 (.134)	[.044] (.137)	[.006] (.029)
1980	[.004] (.015)	.089 (.265)	.053 (.157)	.109 (.301)	.053 (.153)	.117 (.478)
Contrast t	1.618*	.574	1.181	1.983*	.147	1.538
Core service 1960	[.056] (.189)	[.030] (.095)	[.006] (.018)	.005 (.016)	[-.018] (-.054)	[-.042] (-.157)
1980	[.007] (.020)	.006 (.163)	[.017] (.043)	.065 (.163)	[.024] (.063)	[.085] (.294)
Contrast t	1.766*	.793	.295	1.713*	1.081	1.619
Intercept 1960	5.611	6.453	6.819	6.838	6.907	6.650
1980	6.325	6.845	7.189	7.080	7.233	6.555
Adjusted R² 1960	.201	.121	.131	.195	.208	.135
1980	.119	.117	.109	.122	.118	.047
N 1960	5,261	4,444	5,104	4,322	2,583	833
1980	12,665	12,617	8,341	6,592	4,788	1,450

Source: U. S. Bureau of the Census, public use files (one-in-one thousand sample) of the Censuses of Population and Housing, 1960 and of the Census of Population and Housing, 1980 (A sample).

Note: Data are for private-sector workers in nonextractive industries with annual earnings greater than $0 (1959 constant dollars). The standardized coefficients appear without parentheses and are all significant at the .05 level unless enclosed in square brackets. The metric coefficients are in parentheses. The contrast t is the t statistic of the differences in the metric coefficients in 1960 and 1980.

aExcluded category is periphery transformative sector.

*Significance at the .05 level.

sector for otherwise comparable young people in 1980. The analysis of earnings by sex indicates that this pattern holds true for young men, but that young women do not gain significantly from employment in either the core transformative or core service sector compared with employment in periphery transformative industries. Young women do well to avoid employment in periphery services.

The only significant change in the effects of sector occurred for middle-aged (45 to 54 years old) workers. For them, the earnings penalty associated with periphery service employment was reduced, while core transformative employment became more beneficial. This situation helps account for the more peaked shape of the age-earnings profile for all workers (see figure 6.1) and for workers in core sectors (see figure 6.2).

Sex differences for age groups also shed light on the issue of power and sectors. The strong negative effect of employment in periphery services was smaller in 1980 than in 1960 for every age group of women except those 35 to 44 years old, although it remained quite detrimental to earnings (see table 6.9). The effect of employment in the core sectors did not change except for women aged 45 to 54, for whose earnings core transformative- and core service-sector employment became more important. Overall, the earnings prospects for women in core services are not much better than they would be in periphery transformative industries and are not so good as in core transformative industries.

Men had sectoral experiences different from those of women (compare tables 6.8 and 6.9). The negative effects of periphery service employment were considerably smaller for men than they were for women, and the positive effects of core services were considerably larger. Within age categories, there was little change for men in the effect of employment sector on earnings. Most striking is the change in effect of core services for men 55 to 64 years old—employment in this sector was much less beneficial in 1980 than it was for older workers in 1960. This is an indication that the growth of service-sector employment, even in the core, has negative consequences for older men's earnings.

Considering cohort effects. Some may argue, however, that the lower returns for older workers may have been caused by changes in the characteristics of workers (a cohort effect) rather than by structural changes occurring with time (a period effect). That is to say, men 55 to 64 years old in 1980 may not have fared well in 1960 either, but they were then 35 to 44 years old. In table 6.10, I compare the sectoral effects for 1960 and 1980 of men born between 1916 and 1925 (those 55 to 64 years old in 1980) and men born between 1926 and 1935 (those 45 to 54 years old in 1980). Changes in the regression coefficients provide evidence that the decline in the advantage associated with core service employment is caused by changes occurring in the industries. Not only employment in core services has become less beneficial to earnings of the older cohort, so has employment in core transformative industries. Furthermore, periphery service sector employment was more detrimental to these workers' earnings in 1980 than it was when they were younger. The birth cohort that was 45 to 54 years old in 1980 was also worse off in periphery services in 1980 than they were 20 years earlier.

Table 6.10 Changes in Log Earnings Model over Time for Male Birth Cohorts

Variable		Birth Years	
		1926–35[a]	1916–25[b]
Nonwhite	1960	−.477	−.349
	1980	−.262	−.183
	Contrast t	6.329*	3.983*
Education	1960	.042	.064
	1980	.059	.052
	Contrast t	4.007*	3.328*
Professional/	1960	.148	.235
managerial	1980	.253	.341
	Contrast t	3.712*	3.412*
Periphery	1960	.010	−.009
service	1980	−.117	−.232
	Contrast t	2.389*	3.824*
Core	1960	.288	.259
transformative	1980	.236	.162
	Contrast t	1.018	1.719*
Core service	1960	.281	.229
	1980	.196	.067
	Contrast t	1.580	2.738*

Source: U. S. Bureau of the Census, public use files (one-in-one thousand sample) of the *Censuses of Population and Housing, 1960* and of the *Census of Population and Housing, 1980* (A sample).
Note: Figures are metric coefficients.
[a]Age 25–34 in 1960 and 45–54 in 1980.
[b]Age 35–44 in 1960 and 55–64 in 1980.
*Significance at .05 level.

SUMMARY: NEW RULES

Data presented in this chapter suggest that rules guiding the distribution of earnings changed between 1960 and 1980. Overall, the rates of return associated with educational attainment, age, and core sector employment were reduced, and differences within the core between transformative- and service-sector employment increased. This evidence supports my argument that changes in the U.S. postwar economy are reducing resources available to workers.

For men the most dramatic changes occurred within, rather than among, economic sectors. Men in periphery service industries had lower net returns to age and educational attainment over time, but the importance of having a professional, technical, or managerial occupation increased. In core services, the reverse was true, and in core transformative industries, age and occupational advantages were lower in 1980 than in 1960.

These findings do not support the postindustrial theorists' interpretations of the service economy; education and occupation are not more important for earnings in service industries than in transformative industries. The substantial differences between periphery services and core services suggest the importance of organizational features of production not considered in the technical functional theories.

On the other hand, new structuralists have failed to consider the importance of the type of production activity within capital sectors. Differences between transformative and service industries within the core and periphery at each time, as well as differences in the directions of change over time, suggest that type of industry is a dimension of economic organization that should not be neglected. It obviously affects resources available to workers.

For women a major change in the earnings determination process is reduction of the penalty associated with periphery service employment. However, within that sector, returns to age and education were lower in 1980 than in 1960, and a professional, technical, or managerial occupation became relatively more important. Earnings for men and women are distributed according to very different rules. In 1980, only the net effects of employment in core transformative and core service industries did not differ significantly by sex.

In conclusion, my analyses provide limited support for the new segmentation thesis of Gordon, Edwards, and Reich (1982) and Stanback and Noyelle (1982). There does appear to be a change in the segmentation of the labor market along industry lines. However, the declining advantage of employment in the core appears to be caused by improvements in periphery services and by the employment shift within the core toward service industries. The shift toward service employment, and accompanying employment of women, also accounts for much of the increased importance of professional, technical, and managerial occupations. Occupational bifurcation does not appear to be occurring net of these trends (for example, for men within core transformative industries).

In chapter 7, I review the major findings and tie them to theoretical issues posed in previous chapters. I then explore the implications of my findings for theory and policy.

NOTE

1. The different returns by educational level cannot be detected with the continuous variable of educational attainment used in my analysis. However, the continuous variable is useful for considering changes within age groups because of differences in the accessibility of secondary and postsecondary education over time.

7
Social Change and Social Inequality

The 1980s marked the return to social consciousness of a conflict not much pondered since the late 1960s. The new conflict was generational. In the popular press and scholarly journals, writers charged that the young were being excluded from the American dream. The mechanisms of exclusion included high Social Security taxes, high interest rates, and, perhaps most important of all, a constricted, top-heavy labor market. Older workers in blue- and white-collar occupations were envied and despised because they had gained power during a period of economic expansion. During the economic stagnation of the 1970s, their positions were secure.

I presented some of the problems in these popular perceptions in chapter 1, but I argued that the insertion of the issue of power into the study age stratification is useful. Age stratification can be reconceptualized in a way that sees power, not as an individual attribute, but as a structural attribute. In arguing for a political economic theory of old age,

Walker (1981) criticizes functionalist assumptions of homogeneity within the elderly population. Poverty in old age, he argues, is primarily a function of low economic and social status prior to retirement and secondarily a function of the relatively low level of state benefits. Thus, understanding the social relationship between age and the labor market is crucial to understanding the needs of the elderly population. It also contributes to an understanding of the resources available to workers in economic sectors and can be used to study the changes in those resources.

To understand the relationship between social change and social inequality, I have focused on change in capitalist production and outcomes for various groups of workers. I began by accepting evidence provided by new structuralists that, net of individual attributes, workers' earnings are influenced by their participation in capital sectors of industries. To the dual economy model I added industrial sectors defined by type of product: goods or services. The outcomes with which I have been concerned are annual earnings of workers in 1959 and 1979, a period of dramatic change in production.

Unlike other studies in the new structuralist tradition, mine has not attempted to prove the importance of economic segmentation. Instead I have looked for ways in which the influence of economic segmentation and other factors, such as occupation and education, have changed. I have taken the changes in these factors as indicative of changes in the resources available to workers and owners in their struggle with each other over the shares in the outcomes of production. Inferring social change from changed outcomes represents one limit to this research, but one shared by the bulk of empirical research in the social sciences. The strength of my study lies in its fit with a plausible theoretical explanation and its ability to rule out random or other causal influences.

To derive confidence for my inferences about changing resources, I looked at annual earnings in a number of ways at two points in time. With 1960 as the baseline, I compared the situation then to that in 1980. I examined outcomes for workers in nonextractive industries, focusing on men and women separately. I compared the relative positions of age groups within economic sectors and the differences in the importance of economic sector to the earnings of age groups. Below I summarize the findings reported in chapter 6.

SUMMARY OF MAJOR FINDINGS

Change in Outcomes

Workers bring to their jobs a variety of characteristics employers find more or less desirable and receive from their employers a variety of more or less desirable outcomes. The neoclassical view of economics holds that workers with characteristics employers value will have an advantage in the exchange of their labor power for wages, benefits, and security. New structuralists have pointed out, however, that not all work settings are equal, and the ability (or willingness) of employers to reward workers' characteristics are, likewise, unequal. Thus, earnings inequality has a structural basis apart from individual characteristics. My analyses of annual earnings in 1960 and 1980 suggest that changes have occurred in the economic value of sectoral employment for certain groups of workers. I first review the changes in the earnings distribution process associated with individual-level or supply-side characteristics and then review the findings pertaining to structural differences.

The workers' characteristics that changed most in the rate of earnings they received were race and sex. The net effects of being female or nonwhite were smaller in 1980 than they were in 1960. However, the rate of return to women's education, occupation, and age did not improve significantly; in fact, the variables of education and age received lower rates of return. Race had a much greater impact on men's earnings than it did on women's; furthermore, sex differences in the effect of race were greater in 1980 than they were in 1960. Although the earnings penalty associated with being nonwhite was generally lower in 1980 than it had been in 1960, there were two exceptions. In core service industries, the effect of race did not change significantly. Also, the analysis of earnings by age group revealed that for the young the penalty of being nonwhite actually increased between 1960 and 1980. Problems of underemployment of nonwhite youth in modern times seem responsible for this phenomenon.

The relative importance of occupation and education changed during the twenty-year period. In 1960, for nearly every group examined, educational attainment was more important to earnings than was having a professional, technical, or managerial occupation. In 1980, however, for workers under age 45, for those in periphery service industries, and for women, occupation was relatively more important than educational attainment. In most cases, this was because of the lower rates of return to education in 1980. The devaluing of education reflects the use of educational attainment as a screening device to allocate individuals to places in production or to keep them from participation at all.

Another important change since 1960 is the reduced ability of human capital and structural variables to account for the variation in workers' earnings. The only major exception to this trend appeared in the analysis of earnings for workers in the core service sector, where the variance explained by the demographic (human capital) variables was as great in 1980 as in 1960. The higher explanatory power of demographic variables in core services is consistent with conclusions drawn by Pfeffer (1977). He argues that in work settings where productivity is difficult to assess—in staff positions, small organizations, and nonmanufacturing firms (specifically finance, banking, insurance, and real estate)—social status background and contact networks have a greater influence on wages than they do in settings where objective measures of performance are readily available. Sex and race are related to contact networks, and education is correlated with social status background. The work settings Pfeffer describes are found largely in the core service sector.

The analysis for age groups (especially of the labor force taken as a whole and of men) showed considerable reductions in the explanatory power of the dual economy model. The new structuralist framework is less useful in explaining earnings of workers in 1980 than in the past, though it continues to do a better job of accounting for men's earnings than women's. It appears that the resources associated with capital segmentation (market concentration, profit levels, bureaucratic organization, and production activity) are favoring workers less now than in the past.

Changing Conditions of Employment

The basic thesis of the new structuralist perspective is that resources of employers condition the rate of return to workers' characteristics. In previous chapters, I argued that the economy can be divided into sectors based on similarities among industries in what is produced and in how production is organized. I believe that a particularly important finding of this study is the documentation of significant differences for earnings of industry type within core and periphery sectors. Service employment dominates in the periphery; despite this fact, most discussions of the dual economy describe the periphery in terms of its manufacturing industries. The periphery is generally considered the supplier network or the competitive fringe of manufacturers, but it is also composed of many types of services—retail sales, entertainment and recreation, and personal services. Workers in periphery services receive lower earnings than do comparable workers in the periphery transformative industries. This is partially because of the high rate of part-time or part-year employment in periphery services, but even among year-round, full-time workers, industry differences within the periphery are significant (see appendix C).

The earnings associated with periphery service employment have improved since 1960, especially for women. One factor influencing this improvement may be the declining numbers of domestic workers. Some have argued that the rise of services (especially consumer services) represents the shift from women's unpaid production in the home to the provision of domestic goods and services in the market (see Offe 1985). The decline of domestic workers accompanied this shift. Work formerly done in the home is now provided by day-care centers, fast-food establishments, the prepared-food industry, and cleaning and lawn-care services. Although the benefits of these changes for women's unpaid labor are debatable, the decline of domestic labor has put some service workers out of the realm of private, individual wage negotiation into the realm of public protections afforded by minimum-wage laws. Despite these improvements, we must remember that it is possible to work year-round, full-time for minimum wage, have one dependent, and still be officially counted among the poor in this country.

Within the periphery service sector, the education and age of men and of women received lower rates of return in 1980 than in 1960. This finding means that improvement in earnings in the periphery service sector cannot be attributed to a tendency for employers to attach more value to human capital characteristics. More likely, the increased public nature of employment in periphery service industries is primarily responsible for the improvement.

In 1980 men and women experienced significantly lower rates of return to employment in core service industries than to employment in core transformative industries. In 1960 the two sectors of the core were not significantly different in their net effects on earnings (except women's earnings). The lower rate of return to core service employment also appeared in the study of age groups; older men and young women had significant reductions in the earnings benefits attributable to core service employment. Core service industries represent vulnerabilities for workers. They are likely to be characterized by extreme bureaucratic, hierarchical organization (think of your bank, for example), but they lack strong seniority provisions and are virtually free of union influence. Most characteristics of workers received lower rates of return in the core service sector than in the core transformative sector in 1960 and in 1980.

Some have argued that advancements in service industries are not likely to come in the form of machine technology; "retooling" therefore involves bringing in new people rather than retraining workers to use new machines (Singelmann 1978). The dramatic decline in the rate of return associated with core service employment for older men suggests increased vulnerability. The significantly higher rates of return to the middle age categories for workers in core services indicates that experience is not being devalued in this sector. Nevertheless, when the whole labor force is considered, the returns to age remain higher in the core transformative sector than in the core service sector. Age, in and of itself, simply does not bring the same rewards to workers (especially women) in core service and core transformative industries.

Relative to other sectors, core transformative industries did not change very much in their influence on earnings; however, the earnings determination process within this sector did change. The age effects are most interesting because of the contrast with the changes in core services.

Workers, especially men, in the core transformative sector received lower rates of return to age in 1980 than they had in 1960; age-related returns in core services had increased. This supports my argument that age was a correlate of worker power in the past but that changes in core manufacturing are reducing the power of workers to attain high rates of return to their characteristics.

Economists associate large cohort size with lower earnings. They argue that the baby-boom cohort of males (those younger than 35 in 1980) suffers from lower earnings relative to older workers because too many highly educated persons came into the labor market at once (see Freeman 1979; and Welch 1979). This helps explain the decreased rate of return to the 25- to 34-year-old age group but does not explain the decreased rates older age groups receive. In fact, given that reasoning, one would expect that in 1980 skilled workers 55 to 64 years old would have been better off relative to workers 45 to 54 than they had been in 1960, because older cohorts in 1980 represented a smaller proportion of the work force than they had in 1960. However, even the relative earnings of older men in comparatively skilled sectors (such as core transformative industries) declined.

THEORETICAL CONTRIBUTIONS

A Study of Age Advantage, Not Aging

Consistent with the functionalist age stratification literature, I have focused on the relative position of age groups in society. I have not tried to develop a theory of aging in postindustrial society; neither have I sought to develop a political economic theory of aging. My focus was not on the process of aging but on the struggle over outcomes of labor force participation. My interest in age groups, and especially in older workers, comes from a belief that age is a correlate of power in advanced capitalism, and that changes in the power of class actors will be reflected in the position of age groups within economic sectors.

In my study the functionalist assumption of homogeneity of age groups has been rejected, as has human capital theorists' treatment of age only as a proxy for work experience and physical stamina. I have added to the new structuralist approach to stratification the assertion that, like education, race, and sex, age has meaning other than those ascribed to it by human capital and status attainment theories.

As a correlate of power in employment, age has accompanied seniority, authority, and promotion in some jobs. In the past many of these jobs were in the core or center economy and were considered men's jobs. Increased skill also came with age where the social and material technologies of production were structured in such a way to encourage it. Of course, earnings did not always reflect these characteristics of jobs; this was true only where workers could assert their power (either as individuals or as members of organizations).

But not all of the class struggle is contained within the production setting. The power of workers has been aided by the apparatus of the state—labor legislation and welfare policies. According to Burawoy (1983, p. 590),

The *generic* character of the factory regime is, therefore, determined independently of the form of the labor process and competitive pressures among firms. It is determined by the dependence of the livelihood of workers on wage employment and the dependence of the latter on performance in the place of work. State social insurance reduces the first dependence, while labor legislation reduces the second. (Emphasis in original.)

Changes in the relationship between the state and the sphere of production, as well as within the production setting, restructure class relations in advanced capitalism. The power of employers and workers in capitalism is never balanced, because the organization of workers is always a second-order one constituted by employment (Offe and Wiesenthal 1980). Nevertheless, the resources available to class actors have changed, and this has meant greater vulnerability for workers. Some of the factors contributing to the restructuring of class relations include increased price competition within industries, increased centralization within the economy, geographic mobility of capital, changing structures of control, and changing skill requirements because of technological change and industrial shifts. In general, these factors are encompassed in the transformation in the what and the how of production.

Focusing on the What and the How of Production

Recently, sociological journals have been crowded with articles assessing the variety of ways economic segmentation affects individuals and groups in society. This represents a shift in sociology from status attainment research, which focuses on the characteristics of individuals and assumes an open market for acquiring and using talents, to research emphasizing the context or structures in which individuals compete for scarce resources. The origin and nature of the constraints on individual economic success continue to be hotly debated by new structuralists; classes, labor markets, workplaces, companies, and industries have all been shown to condition the returns to employment. Perhaps because of their preoccupation with the appropriate level of economic segmentation, new structuralists have generally ignored the organizational changes that accompany the transformation of employment in late capitalism. At least some of these changes can be traced to the deindustrialization of the United States and the concomitant rise of the service economy.

There has been ample evidence in recent years about the false promises of the service economy (see *Business Week* 1986; and Stanback and Noyelle 1982). Services have not freed workers from the degradation of routinized, boring work. Instead, services have brought many more dead-end, low-paying jobs and have, in general, moved the economy toward greater earnings inequality. It is important to emphasize that the growth of services is not part of an inevitable progression of societies nor is it primarily a response to the changing demands of advanced industrial societies (Offe 1985). The rise of the service sector is a reflection of the ongoing class struggle. In part, its growth is an artifact of the decline of manufacturing within the United States, which is itself a response to capital's interest in expanding or protecting profit levels (Bluestone and Harrison 1982). The employment shift to services is not the result of workers leaving manufacturing jobs to take service jobs; service employees have come primarily from the pool of women who previously had not held jobs (Urquhart 1984). The changing industrial structure thus seems to entail increased fragmentation of the working class. Studies focusing only on the earnings of men will fail to capture the character of economic structure, its constraints and resources, and the consequences of its transformation.

Service industries have characteristics that set them apart from manufacturing industries. Many of these characteristics are not required by the nature of service provision but are instead the result of the historical development of services in U.S. capitalism and could change. Much service employment is part-time, nonunionized, sex-segregated, and low-wage. Service work has occurred in small-sized establishments, which lack internal job ladders. Although service jobs certainly can be lost to overseas workers (keypunching, for example), U.S. service companies find barriers to their participation in foreign markets (*Business Week* 1986).

All of these characteristics help justify the four-sector model of economic segmentation I used to analyze earnings differences among workers. This simple characterization captured complex market and organizational features of the economy, and provided insights into the direction of change in workers' earnings. Stressing service employment demands the inclusion of women in the study of earnings, despite the low explanatory power of industry-level analysis for women's earnings, in itself an important finding.

Men and Women: Different Rules

The separate analyses of earnings for men and women affirm what most women know—in the market for labor they are evaluated differently than are men. Education and professional or managerial occupation are more important to the earnings of women than of men, while employment in service industries of the periphery, where women are most concentrated, is more detrimental. Men receive greater returns to age than do women. Despite women's increased involvement as year-round, full-time workers, male-female differences in the earnings process have generally widened.

Other things being equal, employment in core transformative or core service industries does not contribute more to women's earnings than to men's, but even within these sectors, the rate of return to all characteristics except professional, technical, or managerial occupation was lower for women than men. In 1960 and in 1980, women benefited more from employment in core transformative industries than from employment in core services. But, especially for women, it could be said of either core sector, "It's nice work, if you can get it." Unfortunately, women are still less likely than men to find employment in the core, especially in its transformative industries. This may be partially the result of sex segregation by employers and self-selection by women. Some women may seek out work in periphery services because they lack work experience, need the flexibility offered by nontraditional work schedules, or desire part-time employment. However, regarding the latter, we know that women were overrepresented among nonvoluntary part-time workers in 1979 (U.S. Department of Labor 1980, pp. 54–56). Kessler-Harris argues that women's work habits are determined by wages, not vice versa (cited in Pearce 1986). When given good wages, women will give the time.

Despite the changes since 1960, a few occupations still account for most of the employment of women, and women are even more concentrated in periphery service industries. Women's earnings are still distributed according to rules different from men's, despite the increased devotion of women to full-time continuous employment. Earnings inequality between men and women is not being reduced, though the increased importance of professional and managerial occupations to women's earnings suggests that inequality among women may be increasing.

IMPLICATIONS FOR RESEARCH AND POLICY

The New Structuralist Debate

I cannot hope to have resolved the debate over the appropriate level of analysis among new structuralists. Those who emphasize class resources have argued that the correct level of analysis is beneath the level of industries (see Baron and Bielby 1980; Hodson 1983; and Spaeth 1985). My argument is that industry-level analysis also provides valuable insights into class resources. The study of industrial sectors has the added advantage of facilitating an understanding of the effects of changes occurring outside of the workplace. The study of company or workplace organization narrows the focus of new structuralism and tends to neglect the larger social and economic context in which work is structured. Changes in the economy come about not only because of the actions of capitalists and workers; the state is also an actor.

Burawoy (1983) explicitly links the actions of the state to the relationship between workers and capitalists in various settings, providing a historical and cross-national account of the "politics of production." He argues that the emerging form of production relations will be characterized by increased power of capitalists, owing to the mobility of capital and the structure of past relations, which tied the interests of labor to capital. In the contemporary period, workers have less power in the workplace because the "point of reference is no longer primarily the success of the firm from one year to the next but rates of profit that might be earned elsewhere" (Burawoy 1983, p. 603). State intervention becomes less relevant when the logic of accumulation occurs on a world scale. Workers will ultimately be faced with the "irreconcilability" of their interests and capitalism's development.

Similar conclusions about the fate of labor in the age of international capitalism appear in a variety of works by social scientists. Barnet and Müller (1974) see U.S. labor relations becoming like those in the Third World. Bluestone and Harrison (1982) and Piven and Cloward (1982) argue that the Reagan administration's attack on the welfare state is part of an attempt by the capitalist class to further undermine the institutionalized power of the working class. Capitalists find it necessary to turn against welfare state provisions because unions have so little power in the United States; attacking unions will not accomplish much.

The reduced power of labor is likely to be overlooked in studies that focus on the attributes of individuals or positions. Spaeth (1985), for example, focuses on job power—the control over money and personnel—as a determinant of earnings. His findings reinforce conclusions from other studies that a fundamental class cleavage exists between those with authority in the workplace and those with none. Although Spaeth actually measures resources rather than inferring them, he fails to consider resources outside of the workplace. The differences among the vast majority of workers are neglected. Spaeth concludes: "We have been analyzing earnings where the people are. The time has come to start analyzing them where the power, the resources, and the money are" (p. 616). Spaeth's one-sided view of power continues a tradition of neglecting the conflict and struggle inherent in capitalist production relations and of compartmentalizing production and politics.

My study of economic segmentation and age supports the conclusions drawn by those with a broader vision of capitalism and class struggle. Workers do appear to be becoming more vulnerable: once-powerful segments of the working class (especially workers in core transformative industries) receive lower rates of return to their characteristics (especially to age). The implications of these findings for policy also involve moving beyond organizational- and individual-level solutions.

Industrial Policy And Working Class Politics

Unionization and the labor legislation that supported it have been the major avenues used by workers to strengthen their bargaining power with employers. Unionism has provided certain possibilities for labor, increasing the portion of compensation in fringe benefits and reducing the inequality among workers within and between establishments (Freeman and Medoff 1984). But the declining membership in unions (in the mid-1980s only one in five workers belongs to a union) and the increased mobility of capital have reduced the usefulness of this organizational form to workers.

Organized labor is facing a crisis in late capitalism, in part because unions deal primarily with market relations between workers and employers. In this way, the interests of labor are tied to those of capital. Unions cannot change the nature of production relations; only alterations in ownership and control will have that effect. The actions of the state can affect production relations; however, current U.S. industrial and social policies further emphasize the power of the market to resolve economic problems. Corporations and the wealthy are given incentives to expand production, while the poor are coerced into accepting low-wage jobs.

These policies turn liberal solutions on their head but operate within the same assumptions of open opportunity structures and competitive markets. The internationalization of markets for goods and labor may be interpreted as having increased competition in the 1970s, but the increased competition did not mean improvements in the level of living for most workers. Wage gains fell behind price increases and the bottom 60 percent of the population came out losing. Opportunity structures constricted even further as the share of employment in low-paying, part-time service jobs increased. The continued high levels of joblessness hit nonwhites and the young especially hard. Insecurity and vulnerability have increased, but policies emphasizing individualistic, market solutions will not address these most basic problems.

Burawoy (1983) suggests that the internationalization of contemporary capitalism reduces the possibilities for state intervention in the production process. This seems too pessimistic. State policies already condition the character of international capitalism. For example, tax provisions have given U.S. corporations credit for taxes paid to other countries, facilitating the mobility of capital (see Barnet and Müller [1974], and Bluestone and Harrison [1982] for other examples). Certainly policies with the opposite results are also possible.

Harrington (1984, p. 252) summarizes the threat posed by these structural changes and offers a potential solution:

The nation is in a structural economic crisis, the most severe that we have known in almost a century. The overwhelming majority of the nonpoor are . . . threatened by the same massive trends that have done so much to create a new poverty. The programs that are in their interest, above all full employment, are profoundly in the interest of the new poor. At the same time, there is no single group in the country that can, by its own unaided effort, resolve the crisis for itself.

Full employment represents only one solution to the current crisis suggested by leftist thinkers in the United States. Other recommended policies include providing a guaranteed income for all families, making the minimum wage a living wage, designing a worldwide program for economic stimulation, and setting new standards for corporate responsibility (see the essays in Howe [1984], as well as Bluestone and Harrison [1982] and Harrington [1984], for a variety of solutions from the left).

The political climate of the 1980s makes the implementation of any of these policies seem highly unlikely. Perhaps the current trend toward increased inequality, fewer winners and more losers, will have to continue before the irreconcilability of capitalism and workers' interests will become apparent. The generational conflict that emerged in the 1980s is one indication that hard times fragment the working class rather than bring it together. The declining advantages of core-sector employment to workers at both ends of the age continuum affirm that individualistic policies, designed to improve worker attributes of education or skill, will not provide a solution to the uneasiness in late capitalism.

CONCLUSION: THE UNEASINESS

We have now come full circle. What do we know of the nature of the uneasiness, of the public issue underlying the personal troubles? We can conclude that the charges against older workers misrepresent their economic power as an age group; age is not power in the 1980s. Nor is it the correlate of power in the core sector it once was. The uneasiness of younger generations of workers can be traced more appropriately to the increasing power of capital to exploit all workers and to deny them opportunities to develop skills, to bargain collectively, or even to obtain employment. Yet younger workers see older workers as the enemy, holding on to the prized positions, excluding the young.

But older workers cannot be blamed for the obsolescence of human labor through mechanization, for the deskilling of occupations through the rationalization of work, or for the inflation in the market for educational credentials. They are not responsible for the internationalization of production that threatens the jobs and wages of U.S. workers. The structure of work is undergoing changes that reduce the resources available to workers; older workers have already felt the effects, and the young fear them. A sixty-two-year-old meatcutter in Pittsburgh aptly expressed the situation facing the young and the old. He was dismissed from his job of thirty-seven years after the company decided to sell its forty-three Pittsburgh-area supermarkets because their 2,850 employees refused to accept pay cuts, benefit reductions, and other contract changes. Stated the early retiree (quoted in Winter 1984), "I made a good living. I bought my own house, sent my boy through college and gave the girl a nice wedding. But it won't be that way for the younger people who get our jobs."

APPENDIX A: Industries, Detailed Census Codes, and Sectoral Assignment

Table A.1 Industries, Detailed Census Codes, and Sectoral Assignment

Industry	1960 Census Code	1970 Census Code	1980 Census Code
	Periphery Transformative Sector		
Manufacturing			
Lumber and wood products	107–9	107–9	230–41
Furniture and fixtures	118	118	242
Miscellaneous manufacturing	259, 398	259, 398	391, 392
Textile—knitting mills	307	307	132
Textile—floor covering	309	309	141
Textile—miscellaneous	318	318	150
Apparel and related products	319–27	319–27	151–2
Miscellaneous plastics	387	387	212
Tanned, cured, and finished leather	388	388	220

Table A.1 (continued)

Industry	1960 Census Code	1970 Census Code	1980 Census Code
Leather products, except footwear	397	397	222
Utilities			
Water, sanitary, and other utilties	477–9	477–9	470–2
Core Transformative Sector			
Construction	066	067–077	060
Manufacturing			
Stone, clay, and glass products	119–38	119–38	250–62
Metal industries	139–69	139–69	270–91, 300–1
Machinery, except electrical	176–86	177–98	310–32
Electrical machinery, equipment, and supplies	206	199–209	340–50
Transportation equipment	219–36	219–38	351–70
Professional and photographic equipment, watches	246–49	239–57	371–82
Ordinance	--	258	292
Toys, sporting goods	--	--	390
Food and kindred products	268–98	268–98	100–122
Tobacco	299	299	130
Textile—dyeing and finishing	308	308	140
Textile—yarn, thread, fabric mills	317	317	142
Paper and allied products	328–37	328–37	160–62
Printing and publishing	338–39	338–39	171–72
Chemicals and allied products	346–59	347–69	180–92
Petroleum and coal products	377–78	377–78	200–201
Rubber products	379	379	211
Footwear, except rubber	389	389	221
Utilities			
Electric, gas, and steam power	467–69	467–69	460–62
Periphery Service Sector			
Transportation			
Bus service and urban transit, taxicabs	408–9	408–9	401–2
Services incidental to transportation	429	429	432
Wholesale Trade			
Motor vehicles and equipment	507	507	500
Dry goods and apparel	509	509	542
Farm products—new materials	528	528	551

Table A.1 (continued)

Industry	1960 Census Code	1970 Census Code	1980 Census Code
Hardware, plumbing and heating supplies	536	537	521
Not specified electrical, hardware	--	538	522
Petroleum products	558	558	552
Scrap and waste materials	--	559	531
Paper and its products	--	568	540
Furniture and home furnishings	--	--	501
Lumber and construction	--	569	502
Sporting goods, toys, and hobby goods	--	--	510
Miscellaneous wholesale	566, 588	587–88	532, 562–71
Retail Trade	607–98	607–98	580–691
Services			
Real estate	718	718	712
Advertising	727	727	721
Automobile repair	756	757	751
Other business services	736, 766	728–49, 758–59	722–42, 750, 752, 760
Hotels and motels	776	777	762–770
Other personal services	769, 779–98	769, 778–98	761, 771–91
Entertainment and recreation services	807–9	807–9	800–802
Hospitals, convalescent institutions	838	838–39	831–32
Educational services	856	857–68	842–61, 891
Social services, museums, and other nonprofit firms	876–87	869–87	862–81
Core Service Sector			
Transportation and Communications			
Railroads	407	407	400
Trucking service	417	417	410
Warehousing and storage	418	418	411
Water transportation	419	419	420
Air transportation	427	427	421
Pipelines, except natural gas	428	428	422
Communications	447–49	447–49	440–42
Wholesale Trade			
Drugs, chemicals, and allied products	508	508	541
Food and related products	527	527	550
Farm supplies	--	--	561

Table A.1 (continued)

Industry	1960 Census Code	1970 Census Code	1980 Census Code
Electrical goods	--	529	512
Machinery, equipment, and supplies	539	539	530
Metals and minerals	--	557	511
Alcoholic beverages	--	567	560
Services			
Finance and insurance	706–17	707–17	700–711
Offices of physicians, dentists, health practitioners, and health services	826	828–37	812–30
Legal services	849	849	841
Engineering and architectural firms	888	888	882
Accounting and auditing	889	889	890
Miscellaneous professional services	897	897	892
Public administration	907–37	907–37	900–932, 412

Sources: Harley L. Browning and Joachim Singelmann, "The Transformation of the U.S. Labor Force: The Interaction of Industry and Occupation," *Politics and Society* 8 (1978): 481–509; Charles M. Tolbert II, Patrick M. Horan, and E.M. Beck, "The Structure of Economic Segmentation: A Dual Economy Approach," *American Journal of Sociology* 85 (1980): 1095–1116.

Note: 1970 census codes are those used by Tolbert, Horan, and Beck to classify industries into core and periphery sectors. Transformative and service sectors are derived from the classification given by Browning and Singelmann. Extractive industries are excluded.

APPENDIX B: Supplementary Data

Table B.1 Median Annual Earnings of Age Groups by Economic Sector, 1960 and 1980
(as percentage of 45–54-year-olds)

	Periphery Transformative		Periphery Service		Core Transformative		Core Service	
	1960	1980	1960	1980	1960	1980	1960	1980
Total								
25–34	83	89	96	97	94	78	88	75
35–44	90	100	100	103	102	96	100	94
55–64	93	103	89	94	96	96	98	92
Men								
25–34	79	81	93	75	96	78	91	80
35–44	93	95	109	100	106	99	102	99
55–64	86	95	80	84	96	95	95	91

Table B.1 (continued)

| | Periphery Transformative | | Periphery Service | | Core Transformative | | Core Service | |
	1960	1980	1960	1980	1960	1980	1960	1980
Women								
25–34	90	89	67	96	93	92	82	93
34–44	100	100	83	89	100	92	91	93
55–64	105	96	100	89	100	100	103	100
Total YRFT								
25–34	89	95	103	98	96	83	96	81
35–44	92	100	105	110	106	100	102	97
55–64	89	100	87	98	98	100	98	92
Men YRFT								
25–34	85	84	96	81	93	83	90	81
35–44	100	95	104	101	105	100	101	100
55–64	89	94	85	86	95	100	95	95
Women YRFT								
25–34	102	94	100	105	103	103	95	91
35–44	94	100	100	105	109	109	100	94
55–64	98	100	96	97	100	100	108	102

Source: U. S. Bureau of the Census public use files (one-in-one thousand sample) of the *Censuses of Population and Housing, 1960* and of the *Census of Population and Housing, 1980* (A sample).

YRFT = Year-round, full-time labor force

Table B.2 Median Annual Earnings of Age Groups by Economic Sector, 1960 and 1980 (in 1959 constant dollars)

Age Group	Periphery Transformative		Periphery Service		Core Transformative		Core Service	
	1960	1980	1960	1980	1960	1980	1960	1980
Total								
<25	1500	2000	600	1000	2100	2600	2000	2400
25–34	2400	3200	2700	3500	4600	5200	4300	4800
35–44	2600	3600	2800	3700	5000	6400	4900	6000
45–54	2900	3600	2800	3600	4900	6700	4900	6400
55–64	2700	3700	2500	3400	4700	6400	4800	5900
65 +	2300	1750	1100	1400	3100	2200	3900	1900
Men								
<25	1800	2400	800	1200	2200	2800	2200	2400
25–34	3400	4800	4200	4800	5000	6000	5000	6500
35–44	4000	5600	4900	6400	5500	7600	5600	8000
45–54	4300	5900	4500	6400	5200	7700	5500	8100
55–64	3700	5600	3600	5400	5000	7300	5200	7400
65 +	2600	3100	1550	1700	3400	2300	4350	2050
Women								
<25	1100	1800	500	900	1900	2100	2000	2300
25–34	1800	2400	1200	2600	2800	3600	2800	3700
35–44	2000	2700	1500	2400	3000	3600	3100	3700
45–54	2000	2700	1800	2700	3000	3900	3400	4000
55–64	2100	2600	1800	2400	3000	3900	3500	4000
65 +	1200	1400	1000	1200	2000	2000	2600	1800
Total YRFT								
<25	2800	3200	2600	3200	3600	4000	3000	3500
25–34	3400	4200	4000	4800	5000	6000	4900	5800
35–44	3500	4400	4100	5400	5500	7200	5200	7000
45–54	3800	4400	3900	4900	5200	7200	5100	7200
55–64	3400	4400	3400	4800	5100	7200	5000	6600
65 +	3500	4800	3000	3500	4600	5600	4800	6000
Men YRFT								
<25	2900	3900	3000	3400	3900	4400	3900	4300
25–34	4000	5400	4600	5600	5300	6600	5200	6800
35–44	4700	6100	5000	7000	6000	8000	5850	8400
45–54	4700	6400	4800	6950	5700	8000	5800	8400
55–64	4200	6000	4100	6000	5400	8000	5500	8000
65 +	4000	6400*	3600	4300	4900	6400	5200	7500

Table B.2 (continued)

Age Group	Periphery Transformative		Periphery Service		Core Transformative		Core Service	
	1960	*1980*	*1960*	*1980*	*1960*	*1980*	*1960*	*1980*
Women YRFT								
<25	2500	2800	2200	2900	3100	3400	2900	3200
25–34	2600	3000	2700	4000	3500	4300	3600	4300
35–44	2400	3200	2700	4000	3700	4300	3800	4400
45–54	2550	3200	2700	3800	3400	4400	3800	4700
55–64	2500	3200	2600	3700	3400	4400	4100	4800
65 +	2550*	3200*	2000	2900	3500*	4650*	3500	4200

Source: U. S. Bureau of the Census, public use files (one-in-one thousand sample) of the *Censuses of Population and Housing, 1960* and of the *Census of Population and Housing, 1980* (A sample).

YRFT = Year-round, full-time labor force

* Less than 50 observations.

Table B.3 Contrast t Statistic for Differences in Regression Coefficients of Core Sectors, 1960 and 1980

Variable	1960	1980
Female	3.727*	.707
Nonwhite	3.005*	2.731*
Education	4.715*	.832
Professional/managerial	3.096*	2.869*
Age[a]		
25–34	8.981*	1.280
35–44	10.024*	1.812*
45–54	8.068*	2.480*
55–64	7.850*	2.514*
65 +	2.534*	.404

Source: U. S. Bureau of the Census, public use files (one-in-one thousand sample) of the *Censuses of Population and Housing, 1960* and of the *Census of Population and Housing, 1980* (A sample).

Note: See table 6.4 for coefficients.

[a]The excluded age group for 1960 is 14–24; for 1980, 16–24.

*Significance at .05 level.

Table B.4 Zero-Order Correlation Coefficients, 1960 and 1980

	Female	Nonwhite	Education	Professional/ managerial	25–34	35–44	45–54	55–64	65+	Periphery Service	Core Transformative	Core Service	Log Earnings
Female	--	.039	.059	-.046	-.042	-.010	.003	-.016	-.023	.270	-.277	-.025	-.402
Nonwhite	.025	--	-.188	-.093	.029	.018	-.007	-.019	-.015	.099	-.067	-.053	-.141
Education	-.010	-.112	--	.442	.134	.034	-.087	-.167	-.143	.088	-.111	.105	.154
Professional/ managerial	-.023	-.073	.459	--	.050	.027	.015	.000	.007	.120	-.105	.031	.218
25–34	-.005	-.043	.176	.087	--	-.291	-.257	-.197	-.112	-.046	.037	.013	.078
35–44	-.004	.011	.040	.066	-.289	--	-.266	-.204	-.116	-.054	.043	.014	.141
45–54	-.013	.021	-.064	.035	-.255	-.195	--	-.180	-.103	-.016	.019	-.007	.124
55–64	-.016	-.037	-.123	-.004	-.214	-.164	-.145	--	-.079	.002	-.010	.003	.072
65+	-.004	-.019	-.111	-.015	-.112	-.085	-.075	-.063	--	.041	-.042	-.001	-.060
Periphery service	.236	.010	.094	.113	-.044	-.042	-.042	-.019	.040	--	-.597	-.399	-.321
Core transformative	-.258	-.017	-.124	-.129	.013	.021	.030	.020	-.037	-.568	--	-.344	.235
Core service	-.012	-.011	.088	.049	.040	.024	.016	-.001	-.009	-.490	-.314	--	.135
Log earnings	-.315	-.064	.191	.238	.108	.146	.149	.097	-.092	-.281	.195	.139	--

Source: U. S. Bureau of the Census, public use files (one-in-one thousand sample) of the Censuses of Population and Housing, 1960 and of the Census of Population and Housing, 1980 (A sample).
Note: 1960 above the diagonal, 1980 below the diagonal.

138

APPENDIX C: Regression Analyses for Earnings of Year-Round, Full-Time Workers

Figure C.1   Age-Earnings Profiles by Sex, 1960 and 1980.

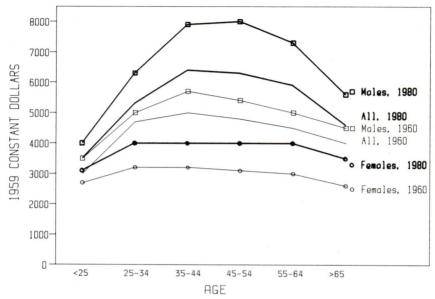

Source: U. S. Bureau of the Census, public use files (one-in-one thousand sample) of the *Censuses of Population and Housing, 1960* and of the *Census of Population and Housing, 1980* (A sample).

Figure C.2   Age-Earnings Profiles by Economic Sector, 1960 and 1980.

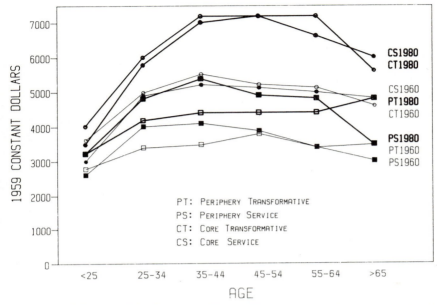

Source: U. S. Bureau of the Census, public use files (one-in-one thousand sample) of the *Censuses of Population and Housing, 1960* and of the *Census of Population and Housing, 1980* (A sample).

Figure C.3   Age-Earnings Profiles of Men by Sector, 1960 and 1980.

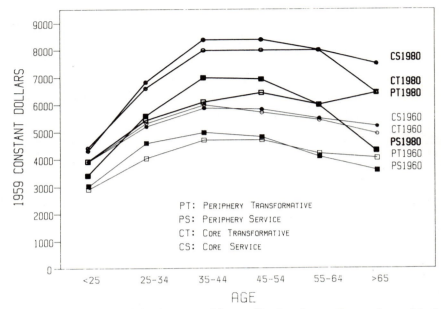

Source: U. S. Bureau of the Census, public use files (one-in-one thousand sample) of the *Censuses of Population and Housing, 1960* and of the *Census of Population and Housing, 1980* (A sample).

Figure C.4   Age-Earnings Profiles of Women by Sector, 1960 and 1980.

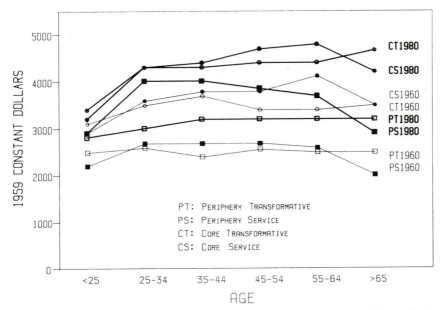

Source: U. S. Bureau of the Census, public use files (one-in-one thousand sample) of the *Censuses of Population and Housing, 1960* and of the *Census of Population and Housing, 1980* (A sample).

Table C.1   Regression of Log Earnings Models, 1960 and 1980

Variable		Model 1	Model 2	Model 3
Female	1960	−.355 (−.476)	−.375 (−.502)	−.352 (−.471)
	1980	−.305 (−.419)	−.317 (−.436)	−.302 (−.415)
	Contrast t			6.074*
Nonwhite	1960	−.155 (−.325)	−.167 (−.349)	−.153 (−.320)
	1980	−.071 (−.135)	−.076 (−.145)	−.070 (−.134)
	Contrast t			16.313*
Education	1960	.248 (.046)	.273 (.051)	.255 (.048)
	1980	.214 (.048)	.226 (.051)	.218 (.049)
	Contrast t			.707
Professional/ managerial	1960	.145 (.215)	.132 (.196)	.148 (.219)
	1980	.133 (.190)	.125 (.178)	.136 (.194)
	Contrast t			2.712*
Age[a]				
25–34	1960	.214 (.300)	.221 (.308)	.215 (.300)
	1980	.215 (.309)	.222 (.319)	.214 (.308)
	Contrast t			.702
35–44	1960	.319 (.428)	.327 (.439)	.319 (.429)
	1980	.295 (.473)	.301 (.484)	.294 (.473)
	Contrast t			3.654*
45–54	1960	.312 (.448)	.317 (.455)	.313 (.450)
	1980	.300 (.516)	.306 (.527)	.300 (.516)
	Contrast t			5.481*
55–64	1960	.242 (.426)	.248 (.437)	.244 (.430)
	1980	.243 (.492)	.245 (.497)	.243 (.492)
	Contrast t			4.608*
65 +	1960	.076 (.279)	.077 (.284)	.077 (.285)
	1980	.049 (.275)	.047 (.263)	.050 (.278)
	Contrast t			.267
Sector				
Core	1960	.210 (.258)	-- --	-- --
	1980	.171 (.230)	-- --	-- --
	Contrast t	3.960*		
Service	1960	-- --	−.126 (−.152)	-- --
	1980	-- --	−.093 (−.128)	-- --
	Contrast t		3.394*	
Periphery service[b]	1960	-- --	-- --	−.073 (−.093)
	1980	-- --	-- --	−.045 (−.062)
	Contrast t			1.993*

Table C.1 (continued)

Variable		Model 1		Model 2		Model 3	
Core	1960	--	--	--	--	.158	(.193)
transformative[b]	1980	--	--	--	--	.132	(.189)
	Contrast t					.257	
Core service[b]	1960	--	--	--	--	.111	(.160)
	1980	--	--	--	--	.107	(.162)
	Contrast t					.129	
Core sector	1960	--	--	--	--	2.121*	
contrast[c]	1980	--	--	--	--	1.736*	
Intercept	1960	7.200		7.653		7.517	
	1980	7.317		7.727		7.586	
Adjusted R^2	1960	.419		.393		.421	
	1980	.325		.305		.325	

Source: U. S. Bureau of the Census, public use files (one-in-one thousand sample) of the *Censuses of Population and Housing, 1960* and of the *Census of Population and Housing, 1980* (A sample).

Note: Data are for private-sector workers in nonextractive industries with annual earnings greater than $0 (1959 constant dollars). The standardized coefficients appear without parentheses and are all significant at the .05 level. The metric coefficients are in parentheses. The contrast t is the t statistic of the differences in the metric coefficients in 1960 and 1980. In 1960, $N = 34,610$; in 1980, $N = 56,840$.

[a]The excluded age group for 1960 is 14–24; for 1980, 16–24.

[b]Relative to the periphery transformative sector.

[c]T statistic for differences between transformative and service sectors of the core.

*Significance at the .05 level.

Table C.2   Regression of Log Earnings Model for Men and Women, 1960 and 1980

Variable		Men	Women	Sex Contrast
Nonwhite	1960	−.171 (−.330)	−.277 (−.152)	2.809*
	1980	−.101 (−.200)	−.048 (−.032)	11.942*
	Contrast t	9.663*	12.474*	
Education	1960	.275 (.044)	.299 (.059)	6.708*
	1980	.233 (.049)	.228 (.049)	.000
	Contrast t	3.536*	3.535*	
Professional/	1960	.170 (.219)	.148 (.229)	.588
managerial	1980	.115 (.159)	.195 (.238)	6.929*
	Contrast t	5.644*	.514	
Age[a]				
25–34	1960	.300 (.366)	.158 (.227)	6.865*
	1980	.264 (.371)	.194 (.236)	9.546*
	Contrast t	.336	.456	
35–44	1960	.436 (.522)	.215 (.275)	12.721*
	1980	.381 (.594)	.216 (.299)	19.844*
	Contrast t	4.843*	1.236	
45–54	1960	.414 (.538)	.239 (.315)	11.485*
	1980	.384 (.642)	.227 (.336)	18.797*
	Contrast t	6.685*	1.050	
55–64	1960	.324 (.515)	.187 (.305)	9.345*
	1980	.304 (.600)	.200 (.343)	14.527*
	Contrast t	5.009*	1.651*	
65 +	1960	.119 (.392)	.027 (.096)	7.671*
	1980	.065 (.355)	.039 (.182)	4.358*
	Contrast t	1.128	1.928*	
Sector[b]				
Periphery service	1960	−.045 (−.054)	−.153 (−.173)	5.169*
	1980	−.052 (−.074)	−.044 (−.049)	1.140
	Contrast t	1.008	4.992*	
Core	1960	.177 (.190)	.159 (.217)	1.132
transformative	1980	.131 (.175)	.139 (.200)	1.140
	Contrast t	.756	.644	
Core service	1960	.116 (.151)	.110 (.146)	.198
	1980	.102 (.155)	.123 (.155)	.000
	Contrast t	.199	.341	
Core sector	1960	2.041*	2.448*	--
contrast[c]	1980	.943	1.989*	--

Table C.2 (continued)

Variable		Men	Women	Sex Contrast
Intercept	1960	7.470	7.057	--
	1980	7.537	7.252	--
Adjusted R^2	1960	.311	.298	--
	1980	.250	.190	--
N	1960	25,107	9,503	--
	1980	35,510	21,330	--

Source: U. S. Bureau of the Census, public use files (one-in-one thousand sample) of the *Censuses of Population and Housing, 1960* and of the *Census of Population and Housing, 1980* (A sample).

Note: Data are for private-sector workers in nonextractive industries with annual earnings greater than $0 (1959 constant dollars). The standardized coefficients appear without parentheses and are all significant at the .05 level. The metric coefficients are in parentheses. The contrast t is the t statistic of the differences in the metric coefficients in 1960 and 1980.

[a]The excluded age group for 1960 is 14–24; for 1980, 16–24.

[b]Relative to the periphery transformative sector.

[c]T statistic for differences between transformative and service sectors of the core.

*Significance at the .05 level.

Table C.3 Regression of Log Earnings Model by Economic Sector, 1960 and 1980

Variable		Periphery		Core	
		Transformative	Service	Transformative	Service
Female	1960	-.350 (-.439)	-.382 (-.537)	-.293 (-.407)	-.389 (-.417)
	1980	-.306 (-.424)	-.292 (-.398)	-.277 (-.420)	-.345 (-.436)
	Contrast t	.482	10.854*	.919	1.412
Nonwhite	1960	-.168 (-.313)	-.183 (-.372)	-.138 (-.285)	-.108 (-.208)
	1980	-.078 (-.140)	-.062 (-.117)	-.090 (-.173)	-.060 (-.110)
	Contrast t	3.997*	13.709*	5.831*	4.414*
Education	1960	.300 (.058)	.248 (.049)	.296 (.048)	.207 (.036)
	1980	.223 (.051)	.218 (.047)	.232 (.053)	.189 (.045)
	Contrast t	1.237	.894	2.236*	3.182*
Professional/ managerial	1960	.168 (.375)	.151 (.232)	.168 (.234)	.152 (.177)
	1980	.167 (.346)	.159 (.219)	.116 (.178)	.119 (.155)
	Contrast t	.538	.822	3.600*	1.556
Age[a] 25–34	1960	.171 (.256)	.203 (.333)	.260 (.297)	.256 (.289)
	1980	.142 (.216)	.211 (.312)	.234 (.322)	.236 (.310)
	Contrast t	.807	.971	1.360	.954
35–44	1960	.275 (.377)	.285 (.449)	.400 (.443)	.374 (.406)
	1980	.201 (.330)	.275 (.461)	.331 (.500)	.331 (.489)
	Contrast t	.950	.540	3.100*	3.661*

		Model 1		Model 2		Model 3		Model 4	
45–54	1960	.308	(.434)	.283	(.464)	.387	(.466)	.353	(.422)
	1980	.225	(.404)	.272	(.486)	.353	(.566)	.325	(.521)
	Contrast t	.581		.932		5.051*		4.367*	
55–64	1960	.247	(.432)	.199	(.390)	.309	(.473)	.311	(.443)
	1980	.206	(.417)	.227	(.464)	.283	(.535)	.252	(.497)
	Contrast t	.262		2.960*		2.923*		2.079*	
65+	1960	.117	(.398)	.051	(.187)	.101	(.386)	.114	(.332)
	1980	.088	(.456)	.029	(.139)	.060	(.421)	.074	(.407)
	Contrast t	.543		1.131		.654		1.524	
Intercept	1960	7.414		7.429		7.678		7.809	
	1980	7.632		7.544		7.706		7.817	
Adjusted R²	1960	.364		.395		.345		.360	
	1980	.281		.285		.286		.327	
N	1960	2,114		11,339		13,466		7,691	
	1980	2,954		21,314		17,996		14,549	

Source: U. S. Bureau of the Census, public use files (one-in-one thousand sample) of the *Censuses of Population and Housing, 1960* and of the *Census of Population and Housing, 1980* (A sample).

Note: Data are for private-sector workers in nonextractive industries with annual earnings greater than $0 (1959 constant dollars). The standardized coefficients appear without parentheses and are all significant at the .05 level. The metric coefficients are in parentheses. The contrast t is the t statistic of the differences in the metric coefficients in 1960 and 1980.

[a]The excluded age group for 1960 is 14–24; for 1980, 16–24.

*Significance at the .05 level.

149

Table C.4 Regression of Log Earnings Model for Men by Economic Sector, 1960 and 1980

	Periphery		Core	
Variable	Transformative	Service	Transformative	Service
Nonwhite				
1960	-.240 (-.432)	-.191 (-.371)	-.155 (-.305)	-.148 (-.253)
1980	-.086 (-.170)	-.091 (-.184)	-.115 (-.221)	-.103 (-.190)
Contrast t	4.410*	7.124*	3.951*	2.341*
Education				
1960	.330 (.063)	.236 (.040)	.319 (.049)	.234 (.034)
1980	.252 (.058)	.200 (.041)	.259 (.056)	.225 (.045)
Contrast t	.707	.354	3.131*	3.889*
Professional/ managerial				
1960	.176 (.356)	.165 (.218)	.176 (.229)	.198 (.201)
1980	.176 (.333)	.133 (.187)	.103 (.152)	.096 (.118)
Contrast t	.357	1.458	4.537*	4.515*
Age[a]				
25–34				
1960	.188 (.286)	.291 (.400)	.316 (.351)	.372 (.380)
1980	.174 (.272)	.269 (.401)	.261 (.352)	.313 (.397)
Contrast t	.211	.034	.047	.522
35–44				
1960	.347 (.495)	.396 (.549)	.473 (.513)	.525 (.520)
1980	.243 (.421)	.372 (.630)	.385 (.569)	.462 (.640)
Contrast t	1.100	2.715*	2.553*	3.770*

		(1)	(2)	(3)	(4)
45–54	1960	.346 (.516)	.363 (.541)	.459 (.540)	.487 (.537)
	1980	.290 (.546)	.352 (.655)	.407 (.634)	.455 (.674)
	Contrast t	.424	3.649*	4.286*	4.121*
55–64	1960	.287 (.517)	.247 (.444)	.367 (.544)	.424 (.548)
	1980	.256 (.547)	.280 (.594)	.329 (.607)	.340 (.620)
	Contrast t	.382	4.404*	2.545*	1.996*
65+	1960	.148 (.463)	.086 (.280)	.121 (.442)	.175 (.449)
	1980	.109 (.562)	.050 (.234)	.056 (.408)	.099 (.485)
	Contrast t	.707	.803	.534	.579
Intercept	1960	7.322	7.469	7.607	7.730
	1980	7.485	7.538	7.634	7.719
Adjusted R²	1960	.357	.271	.298	.243
	1980	.209	.233	.240	.205
N	1960	1,373	6,852	11,417	5,465
	1980	1,708	11,001	14,023	8,778

Source: U. S. Bureau of the Census, public use files (one-in-one thousand sample) of the *Censuses of Population and Housing, 1960* and of the *Census of Population and Housing, 1980* (A sample).

Note: Data are for private-sector workers in nonextractive industries with annual earnings greater than $0 (1959 constant dollars). The standardized coefficients appear without parentheses and are all significant at the .05 level. The metric coefficients are in parentheses. The contrast t is the t statistic of the differences in the metric coefficients in 1960 and 1980.

[a]The excluded age group for 1960 is 14–24; for 1980, 16–24.

[b]Relative to the periphery transformative sector.

[c]T statistic for differences between transformative and service sectors of the core.

*Significance at the .05 level.

Table C.5 Regression of Log Earnings Model for Women by Economic Sector, 1960 and 1980

Variable		Periphery		Core	
		Transformative	Service	Transformative	Service
Nonwhite	1960	[.039] (.062)	−.199 (−.352)	−.067 (−.122)	[−.032] (−.060)
	1980	−.097 (−.123)	−.036 (−.056)	[−.019] (−.028)	[−.010] (−.014)
	Contrast t	2.801*	10.993*	2.116*	1.130
Education	1960	.234 (.037)	.334 (.067)	.222 (.034)	.199 (.044)
	1980	.194 (.037)	.261 (.053)	.165 (.038)	.163 (.042)
	Contrast t	0.000	3.883*	.800	.343
Professional/ managerial	1960	.148 (.371)	.153 (.236)	.148 (.252)	.075 (.090)
	1980	.145 (.306)	.197 (.239)	.168 (.248)	.189 (.210)
	Contrast t	.604	.116	.091	4.188*
Age[a]					
25–34	1960	.143 (.159)	.156 (.272)	.148 (.135)	.241 (.244)
	1980	.119 (.138)	.177 (.230)	.208 (.236)	.247 (.263)
	Contrast t	.295	1.204	2.796*	.628
35–44	1960	.124 (.121)	.218 (.331)	.213 (.175)	.316 (.298)
	1980	.159 (.194)	.200 (.296)	.217 (.274)	.270 (.338)
	Contrast t	1.050	1.041	2.745*	1.307

45–54	1960	.243 (.237)	.250 (.377)	.188 (.170)	.317 (.318)
	1980	.152 (.205)	.217 (.332)	.249 (.341)	.255 (.358)
	Contrast t	.448	1.318	4.478*	1.225
55–64	1960	.155 (.198)	.187 (.333)	.152 (.187)	.290 (.362)
	1980	.151 (.224)	.195 (.342)	.193 (.305)	.231 (.396)
	Contrast t	.324	.242	2.646*	.903
65+	1960	[.060] (.215)	[.019] (.065)	.062 (.217)	.075 (.205)
	1980	.068 (.277)	[.011] (.049)	.082 (.401)	.080 (.417)
	Contrast t	.351	.250	1.712*	2.474*
Intercept	1960	7.320	6.759	7.625	7.373
	1980	7.476	7.145	7.585	7.468
Adjusted R^2	1960	.097	.299	.098	.139
	1980	.090	.202	.109	.162
N	1960	741	4,487	2,049	2,226
	1980	1,246	10,340	3,973	5,771

Source: U. S. Bureau of the Census, public use files (one-in-one thousand sample) of the Censuses of Population and Housing, 1960 and of the Census of Population and Housing, 1980 (A sample).

Note: Data are for private-sector workers in nonextractive industries with annual earnings greater than $0 (1959 constant dollars). The standardized coefficients appear without parentheses and are all significant at the .05 level unless enclosed in square brackets. The metric coefficients are in parentheses. The contrast t is the t statistic of the differences in the metric coefficients in 1960 and 1980.

[a]The excluded age group for 1960 is 14–24; for 1980, 16–24.

*Significance at the .05 level.

Table C.6 Regression of Log Earnings Model for Workers by Age Group, 1960 and 1980

Variable		<25	25–34	35–44	45–54	55–64	65 +
Female	1960	−.228 (−.274)	−.332 (−.425)	−.416 (−.535)	−.396 (−.518)	−.360 (−.495)	−.322 (−.547)
	1980	−.184 (−.220)	−.293 (−.355)	−.369 (−.510)	−.376 (−.524)	−.339 (−.477)	−.203 (−.350)
	Contrast t	2.346*	4.854*	1.768*	.354	.847	7.160*
Nonwhite	1960	−.160 (−.321)	−.188 (−.329)	−.156 (−.302)	−.158 (−.339)	−.142 (−.342)	−.096 (−.258)
	1980	−.056 (−.098)	−.078 (−.125)	−.076 (−.139)	−.081 (−.165)	−.079 (−.176)	[.003] (.008)
	Contrast t	6.221*	10.507*	7.944*	7.005*	4.662*	1.848*
Education	1960	.187 (.051)	.248 (.044)	.284 (.052)	.260 (.048)	.254 (.046)	.185 (.036)
	1980	.112 (.034)	.191 (.041)	.247 (.054)	.250 (.052)	.240 (.050)	.227 (.050)
	Contrast t	3.400*	1.061	.707	1.414	1.414	1.519
Professional/ managerial	1960	.050 (.091)	.113 (.140)	.143 (.196)	.209 (.311)	.196 (.313)	.199 (.347)
	1980	.097 (.147)	.120 (.146)	.153 (.211)	.150 (.212)	.177 (.265)	.167 (.301)
	Contrast t	1.666*	.366	.884	4.988*	11.924*	.580
Sector[a]							
Periphery service	1960	−.107 (−.132)	[−.016] (−.018)	−.044 (−.055)	−.088 (−.110)	−.121 (−.157)	−.201 (−.304)
	1980	−.095 (−.115)	[−.007] (−.009)	[−.012] (−.016)	−.037 (−.052)	−.069 (−.097)	−.290 (−.487)
	Contrast t	.385	.310	1.280	1.703*	1.369	1.374

154

Core transformative	1960	.153	(.187)	.197	(.210)	.117	(.205)	.142	(.173)	.159	(.205)	[.089]	(.154)
	1980	.102	(−.131)	.163	(.207)	.154	(.218)	.147	(.208)	.118	(.171)	[.010]	(.022)
	Contrast t	1.249		.138		.436		1.028		.776		.933	
Core service	1960	.085	(.120)	.148	(.186)	.116	(.157)	.084	(.123)	.119	(.176)	[.064]	(.113)
	1980	.053	(.075)	.143	(.188)	.137	(.204)	.109	(.168)	.079	(.128)	[.002]	(.005)
	Contrast t	.957		.066		1.542		1.296		1.061		.761	
Intercept	1960	7.441		7.839		7.901		7.986		7.971		8.011	
	1980	7.749		7.968		7.991		8.089		8.103		8.068	
Adjusted R^2	1960	.198		.351		.454		.441		.416		.337	
	1980	.094		.210		.338		.349		.324		.264	
N	1960	3,631		8,350		9,417		7,688		4,592		932	
	1980	8,592		17,577		12,468		10,373		7,001		839	

Source: U. S. Bureau of the Census, public use files (one-in-one thousand sample) of the *Censuses of Population and Housing, 1960* and of the *Census of Population and Housing, 1980* (A sample).

Note: Data are for private-sector workers in nonextractive industries with annual earnings greater than $0 (1959 constant dollars). The standardized coefficients appear without parentheses and are all significant at the .05 level unless enclosed in square brackets. The metric coefficients are in parentheses. The contrast t is the t statistic of the differences in the metric coefficients in 1960 and 1980.

aExcluded category is periphery transformative sector.
*Significance at the .05 level.

Table C.7 Regression of Log Earnings Model for Men within Age Groups, 1960 and 1980

Variable		<25	25–34	35–44	45–54	55–64	65+
Nonwhite	1960	−.171 (−.327)	−.200 (−.338)	−.185 (−.319)	−.169 (−.331)	−.158 (−.335)	−.145 (−.336)
	1980	−.072 (−.133)	−.111 (−.182)	−.133 (−.242)	−.134 (−.264)	−.080 (−.176)	[.011] (.030)
	Contrast t	4.213*	6.444*	3.025*	2.105*	3.625*	2.691*
Education	1960	.183 (.045)	.256 (.039)	.340 (.051)	.283 (.045)	.266 (.042)	.171 (.029)
	1980	.117 (.036)	.186 (.038)	.290 (.055)	.284 (.051)	.270 (.050)	.252 (.053)
	Contrast t	1.273	.354	1.411	2.121*	1.886*	2.105*
Professional/ managerial	1960	.080 (.134)	.124 (.136)	.164 (.184)	.249 (.326)	.237 (.323)	.240 (.364)
	1980	.059 (.099)	.092 (.110)	.139 (.177)	.136 (.176)	.190 (.262)	.158 (.280)
	Contrast t	.814	1.361	.353	6.239*	2.006*	.871
Sector[a]							
Periphery service	1960	[−.056] (−.068)	[.040] (.042)	[−.033] (−.037)	−.067 (−.081)	−.109 (−.132)	−.179 (−.142)
	1980	−.107 (−.139)	[−.014] (−.018)	[.002] (.003)	−.054 (−.075)	−.102 (−.142)	−.314 (−.537)
	Contrast t	1.223	1.601	1.020	.134	.179	1.721*

Core transformative	1960	.162 (.184)	.246 (.234)	.186 (.180)	.168 (.180)	.191 (.208)	[.106] (.153)
	1980	.096 (.122)	.165 (.194)	.186 (.234)	.144 (.181)	.115 (.150)	[−.045] (−.096)
	Contrast t	1.095	1.088	1.428	.023	1.063	1.404
Core service	1960	.084 (.133)	.184 (.210)	.112 (.128)	.094 (.123)	.137 (.175)	[.086] (.132)
	1980	.052 (.088)	.147 (.192)	.164 (.228)	.112 (.157)	.062 (.093)	[−.045] (−.088)
	Contrast t	.697	.480	2.551*	.748	1.429	1.258
Intercept	1960	7.485	7.862	7.930	7.995	7.999	8.053
	1980	7.747	8.038	7.980	8.142	8.130	8.113
Adjusted R²	1960	.146	.210	.286	.297	.289	.232
	1980	.061	.102	.195	.190	.197	.195
N	1960	2,239	6,555	6,928	5,423	3,279	683
	1980	4,791	11,074	8,050	6,655	4,427	513

Source: U. S. Bureau of the Census, public use files (one-in-one thousand sample) of the *Censuses of Population and Housing, 1960* and of the *Census of Population and Housing, 1980* (A sample).

Note: Data are for private-sector workers in nonextractive industries with annual earnings greater than $0 (1959 constant dollars). The standardized coefficients appear without parentheses and are all significant at the .05 level unless enclosed in square brackets. The metric coefficients are in parentheses. The contrast t is the t statistic of the differences in the metric coefficients in 1960 and 1980.

ªThe excluded age group for 1960 is 14–24; for 1980, 16–24.

*Significance at the .05 level.

Table C.8   Regression of Log Earnings Model for Women within Age Groups, 1960 and 1980

Variable		<25		25–34		35–44		45–54		55–64		65+	
Nonwhite	1960	-.146	(-.300)	-.186	(-.268)	-.148	(-.243)	-.184	(-.342)	-.145	(-.342)	[.027]	(.081)
	1980	-.032	(-.050)	-.039	(-.050)	[-.001]	(-.002)	[-.020]	(-.032)	-.101	(-.181)	[-.006]	(-.013)
	Contrast t	4.402*		6.677*		6.841*		7.552*		2.477*		.477	
Education	1960	.212	(.068)	.324	(.065)	.286	(.056)	.309	(.054)	.310	(.057)	.292	(.063)
	1980	.094	(.028)	.234	(.047)	.232	(.049)	.271	(.054)	.245	(.049)	.205	(.045)
	Contrast t	3.885*		3.087*		1.400		0.000		1.249		.976	
Professional/ managerial	1960	[.012]	(.023)	.136	(.188)	.168	(.244)	.197	(.274)	.171	(.287)	.166	(.318)
	1980	.158	(.203)	.189	(.203)	.229	(.272)	.223	(.272)	.198	(.270)	.204	(.351)
	Contrast t	3.087*		.429		.887		.058		.329		.220	
Sector[a]													
Periphery service	1960	-.199	(-.233)	-.181	(-.189)	-.091	(-.097)	-.144	(-.154)	-.159	(-.198)	-.334	(-.543)
	1980	-.078	(-.082)	[-.008]	(-.009)	[-.039]	(-.043)	[-.037]	(-.041)	[-.036]	(-.042)	-.270	(-.401)
	Contrast t	2.126*		3.584*		1.123		2.251*		2.190*		.536	

	1960	1980	Contrast t	1960	1980	Contrast t	1960	1980	Contrast t	1960	1980	Contrast t	1960	1980	Contrast t	1960	1980	Contrast t
Core transformative	.155 (.216)	.105 (.143)	.989	.145 (.175)	.168 (.225)	.969	.227 (.280)	.142 (.199)	1.590	.133 (.176)	.170 (.243)	1.246	.128 (.215)	.117 (.175)	.509	[.086] (.226)	[.116] (.236)	.033
Core service	[.060] (.073)	.072 (.083)	.140	.102 (.123)	.158 (.180)	1.099	.166 (.213)	.140 (.176)	.726	.095 (.125)	.125 (.163)	.707	.115 (.176)	.123 (.177)	.013	[−.023] (−.045)	[.090] (.172)	.756
Intercept 1960	7.020			7.238			7.299			7.425			7.391			7.346		
Intercept 1980	7.574			7.486			7.512			7.489			7.598			7.653		
Adjusted R² 1960	.181			.323			.293			.319			.304			.231		
Adjusted R² 1980	.064			.151			.167			.197			.190			.218		
N 1960	1,392			1,795			2,489			2,265			1,313			249		
N 1980	3,801			6,503			4,418			3,718			2,574			316		

Source: U. S. Bureau of the Census, public use files (one-in-one thousand sample) of the *Censuses of Population and Housing, 1960* and of the *Census of Population and Housing, 1980* (A sample).

Note: Data are for private-sector workers in nonextractive industries with annual earnings greater than $0 (1959 constant dollars). The standardized coefficients appear without parentheses and are all significant at the .05 level unless enclosed in square brackets. The metric coefficients are in parentheses. The contrast t is the t statistic of the differences in the metric coefficients in 1960 and 1980.

^aThe excluded age group for 1960 is 14–24; for 1980, 16–24.

*Significance at the .05 level.

Bibliography

Aldrich, Howard, and Jane Weiss. 1981. "Differentiation within the United States Capitalist Class: Workforce Size and Income Differences." *American Sociological Review* 46:279–90.

Alsop, Ronald. 1984. "Mixed Bag: As Early Retirement Grows in Popularity, Some Have Misgivings." *Wall Street Journal*, April 24, 1.

Althauser, Robert P., and Arne L. Kalleberg. 1981. "Firms, Occupations, and the Structure of Labor Markets: A Conceptual Analysis." In *Sociological Perspectives on Labor Markets*, edited by Ivar E. Berg, 119–49. New York: Academic Press.

Averitt, Robert T. 1968. *The Dual Economy: The Dynamics of American Industry Structure*. New York: Norton.

Babson, Steve. 1973. "The Multinational Corporation and Labor." *Review of Radical Political Economics* 5:19–36.

Bain, Joe S. 1968. *Industrial Organization*. 2d ed. New York: Wiley.

Baran, Paul A., and Paul M. Sweezy. 1966. *Monopoly Capital: An Essay on the American Economic and Social Order*. New York: Modern Reader Paperbacks.

Barnet, Richard J., and Ronald E. Müller. 1974. *Global Reach: The Power of the Multinational Corporations*. New York: Simon and Schuster.

Baron, James N., and William T. Bielby. 1980. "Bringing the Firms Back In: Stratification and the Organization of Work." *American Sociological Review* 45:737–65.

Beck, E. M. 1980. "Labor Unionism and Racial Income Inequality: A Time-Series Analysis of the Post–World War II Period." *American Journal of Sociology* 85:791–814.

Beck, E. M., Patrick M. Horan, and Charles M. Tolbert II. 1980. "Industrial Segmentation and Labor Market Discrimination." *Social Problems* 28:113–30.

———. 1978. "Stratification in a Dual Economy: A Sectoral Model of Earnings Determination." *American Sociological Review* 43:704–20.

Becker, Gary S. 1971. *Economic Theory*. Alfred A. Knopf Books in Economics. New York: Knopf.

Bell, Daniel. 1976. *The Coming of Post-Industrial Society: A Venture in Social Forecasting*. 2d ed. New York: Basic Books.

Bibb, Robert, and William H. Form. 1977. "The Effects of Industrial, Occupational, and Sex Stratification on Wages in Blue-Collar Markets." *Social Forces* 55:974–96.

Blau, Peter M., and Otis Dudley Duncan. 1967. *The American Occupational Structure*. New York: Wiley.

Blau, Peter M., Cecilia McHugh Falbe, William McKinley, and Phelps K. Tracy. 1976. "Technology and Organization in Manufacturing." *Administrative Science Quarterly* 21:20–40.

Blauner, Robert. 1964. *Alienation and Freedom: The Factory Worker and His Industry*. Chicago: University of Chicago Press.

Bluestone, Barry, Patricia Hanna, Sarah Kuhn, and Laura Moore. 1981. *The Retail Revolution: Market Transformation, Investment, and Labor in the Modern Department Store*. Boston: Auburn House.

Bluestone, Barry, and Bennett Harrison. 1982. *The Deindustrialization of America: Plant Closings, Community Abandonment, and the Dismantling of Basic Industry*. New York: Basic Books.

Bluestone, Barry, William M. Murphy, and Mary Stevenson. 1973. *Low Wages and the Working Poor*. Policy Papers in Human Resources and Industrial Relations, no. 22. Ann Arbor: Institute of Labor and Industrial Relations, University of Michigan–Wayne State University.

Blumberg, Paul. 1980. *Inequality in an Age of Decline*. Oxford: Oxford University Press.

Bonacich, Edna. 1976. "Advanced Capitalism and Black/White Race Relations in the United States: A Split Labor Market Interpretation." *American Sociological Review* 41:34–51.

———. 1972. "A Theory of Ethnic Antagonism: The Split Labor Market. *American Sociological Review* 37:547–59.

Bowles, Samuel, and Herbert Gintis. 1976. *Schooling in Capitalist America: Educational Reform and the Contradictions of Economic Life*. New York: Basic Books.
———. 1975. "The Problem with Human Capital Theory—A Marxian Critique." *American Economic Review* 65:74–82.
Braverman, Harry. 1974. *Labor and Monopoly Capital: The Degradation of Work in the Twentieth Century*. New York: Monthly Review Press.
Brennan, Michael J., Phillip Taft, and Mark B. Schupack. 1967. *The Economics of Age*. New York: Norton.
Brooks, Geraldine. 1983. "Faced with a Changing Work Force, TRW Pushes to Raise White-Collar Productivity." *Wall Street Journal*, September 22, 33.
Browning, Harley L., and Joachim Singelmann. 1978. "The Transformation of the U.S. Labor Force: The Interaction of Industry and Occupation." *Politics and Society* 8:481–509.
Burawoy, Michael. 1983. "Between the Labor Process and the State: The Changing Face of Factory Regimes under Advanced Capitalism." *American Sociological Review* 48:587–605.
———. 1982. "Introduction: The Resurgence of Marxism in American Sociology." In *Marxist Inquiries*, edited by Michael Burawoy and Theda Skocpol, S1–S30. Chicago: University of Chicago Press.
———. 1977. "Social Structure, Homogenization, and 'The process of Status Attainment in the United States and Great Britain'." *American Journal of Sociology* 82:1031–42.
Business Week. 1986. "Special Report: The Hollow Corporation." March 3, 57–85.
Cain, Glen C. 1976. "The Challenge of Segmented Labor Market Theories to Orthodox Theory: A Survey." *Journal of Economic Literature* 14:1215–57.
Calhoun, Craig Jackson. 1983. "The Radicalism of Tradition: Community Strength or Venerable Disguise and Borrowed Language?" *American Journal of Sociology* 88:886–914.
Carey, Max L. 1981. "Occupational Employment Growth through 1990." *Monthly Labor Review* 104(8):42–55.
Clark, Robert, Juanita Kreps, and Joseph Spengler. 1978. "Economics of Aging: A Survey." *Journal of Economic Literature* 16:919–62.
Colclough, Glenna, and Patrick M. Horan. 1983. "The Status Attainment Paradigm: The Application of a Kuhnian Perspective." *Sociological Quarterly* 24:25–42.
Collins, Randall. 1979. *The Credential Society: An Historical Sociology of Education and Stratification*. New York: Academic Press.
Cowgill, Donald O. 1986. *Aging Around the World*. Belmont, Calif.: Wadsworth.
———. 1972. "A Theory of Aging in Cross-Cultural Perspective." In *Aging and Modernization*, edited by Donald O. Cowgill and Lowell D. Holmes, 1–14. Sociology Series. New York: Appleton-Century-Crofts.
Davis, Kingsley, and Wilbert E. Moore. 1945. "Some Principles of Stratification." *American Sociological Review* 10:242–49.
Davis, Kingsley, and Pietronella van den Oever. 1981. "Age Relations and Public Policy in Advanced Industrial Societies." *Population and Development Review* 7:1–18.
Doeringer, Peter B., and Michael J. Piore. 1971. *Internal Labor Markets and Man-*

power Analysis. Lexington, Mass.: Heath.

Dooley, Martin, and Peter Gootschalk. 1982. "Does a Younger Male Labor Force Mean Greater Earnings Inequality?" *Monthly Labor Review* 105(12): 42–45.

Dowd, James J. 1980. *Stratification among the Aged*. Brooks/Cole Series in Social Gerontology. Monterey, Calif.: Brooks/Cole.

Drucker, Peter F. 1982. "Are Unions Becoming Irrelevant?" *Wall Street Journal*, September 22, 30.

Duncan, Otis Dudley. 1968. "Social Stratification and Mobility: Problems in the Measurement of Trend." In *Indicators of Social Change: Concepts and Measurements*, edited by Eleanor B. Sheldon and Wilbert E. Moore, 675–719. New York: Russell Sage Foundation.

Dunlop, John T. 1966. "Job Vacancy Measures and Economic Analysis." In *The Measurement and Interpretation of Job Vacancies: A Conference Report of the National Bureau of Economic Research*, 27–47. New York: National Bureau of Economic Research.

———. 1957. "The Task of Contemporary Wage Theory." In *New Concepts in Wage Discrimination*, edited by George William Taylor and Frank C. Pierson, pp. 117–39. New York: McGraw-Hill.

Easterlin, Richard A., Michael L. Wachter, and Susan Wachter. 1978. "Demographic Influences on Economic Stability: The United States Experience." *Population and Development Review* 4:1–22.

Edwards, Richard C. 1975. "The Social Relations of Production in the Firm and Labor Market Structure." In *Labor Market Segmentation*, edited by Richard C. Edwards, Michael Reich, and David M. Gordon, 3–26. Lexington, Mass.: Heath.

Eisenstadt, S. N. 1966. *Modernization: Protest and Change*. Modernization of Traditional Societies Series. Engelwood Cliffs, N.J.: Prentice-Hall.

English, Carey W., and Richard L. DeLouise. 1983. "Jobs in the '80s—The Changes Taking Shape." *U.S. News and World Report* 95(August 8): 61–62.

Farley, Reynolds. 1984. *Blacks and Whites: Narrowing the Gap?* Cambridge: Harvard University Press.

Featherman, David L., and Robert M. Hauser. 1978. *Opportunity and Change*. New York: Academic Press.

Flagg, Michael. 1983. "Textile Industry Fights Imports." *The News and Observer* (Raleigh, N.C.), December 27, 1D–2D.

Flaim, Paul A., and Ellen Sehgal. 1985. "Displaced Workers of 1979–83: How Well Have They Fared?" *Monthly Labor Review* 108(6): 3–16.

Form, William. 1983. "Sociological Research and the American Working Class." *Sociological Quarterly* 24:163–84.

Freedman, Marcia K. 1976. *Labor Markets: Segments and Shelters*. Conservation of Human Resources Series, Land Mark Studies. Montclair, N.J.: Allanheld, Osmun; Universe Books.

Freeman, Richard B. 1979. "The Effect of Demographic Factors on Age-Earnings Profiles." *Journal of Human Resources* 14:289–318.

Freeman, Richard B., and James L. Medoff. 1984. *What Do Unions Do?* New York: Basic Books.

Friedmann, Harriet. 1981. "The Family Farm in Advanced Capitalism." Paper presented at the American Sociological Association annual meeting, August 24–28, Toronto, Canada.

Fromson, Brett Duval. 1983. "The '70s Were A Decade of the Young . . . Left Behind." *Wall Street Journal*, October 13, 28.

Fuchs, Victor R. 1968. *The Service Economy*. National Bureau of Economic Research General Series, no. 87. New York: National Bureau of Economic Research.

Galbraith, John Kenneth. 1977. "The Technostructure and the Corporation in the New Industrial State." In *American Society, Inc.: Studies of the Social Structure and Political Economy of the United States*, edited by Maurice Zeitlin, 202–14. Chicago: Rand McNally.

———. 1971. *The New Industrial State*. 2d rev. ed. Boston: Houghton Mifflin.

Geewax, Marilyn. 1986. "Many Retirees Face a Financial Rat Race." *Atlanta Journal/Atlanta Constitution*, June 9, 1C.

Giddens, Anthony. 1975. *The Class Structure of the Advanced Societies*. New York: Harper & Row.

Glenn, Evelyn Nakano, and Roslyn L. Feldberg. 1979. "Proletarianizing Clerical Work: Technology and Organizational Control in the Office." In *Case Studies on the Labor Process*, edited by Andrew Zimbalist, pp. 51–72. New York: Monthly Review Press.

Gordon, David M. 1972. *Theories of Poverty and Underemployment: Orthodox, Radical, and Dual Labor Market Perspectives*. Lexington, Mass.: Lexington Books.

Gordon, David M., Richard Edwards, and Michael Reich. 1982. *Segmented Work, Divided Workers: The Historical Transformation of Labor in the United States*. Cambridge: Cambridge University Press.

Gordon, Meryl. 1985. "The High Cost of Low Prices." *New York Times*, August 11, sec. 3, 1.

Granovetter, Mark. 1984. "Small Is Bountiful: Labor Markets and Establishment Size." *American Sociological Review* 49:323–34.

———. 1981. "Toward a Sociological Theory of Income Differences." In *Sociological Perspectives on Labor Markets*, edited by Ivar E. Berg, 11–47. New York: Academic Press.

Harrington, Michael. 1984. *The New American Poverty*. New York: Penguin.

Harris, Roy J., Jr. 1983. "More Firms Set Two-Tier Pay Pacts with Unions, Hurting Future Hires." *Wall Street Journal*, December 15, 33.

Hodson, Randy D. 1984. "Companies, Industries, and the Measurement of Economic Segmentation." *American Sociological Review* 49:335–48.

———. 1983. *Workers' Earnings and Corporate Economic Structure*. New York: Academic Press.

———. 1978. "Labor in the Monopoly, Competitive, and State Sectors of Production." *Politics and Society* 8:429–80.

Hodson, Randy, and Robert L. Kaufman. 1982. "Economic Dualism: A Critical Review." *American Sociological Review* 47:727–39.

———. 1981. "Circularity in the Dual Economy: A Comment on Tolbert, Horan, and Beck." *American Journal of Sociology* 86:881–87.

Hoffman, Saul D. 1981. "On-the-Job Training: Differences by Race and Sex." *Monthly Labor Review* 104(7): 34–36.

Horan, Patrick. 1978. "Is Status Attainment Research Atheoretical?" *American Sociological Review* 43:534–41.

Horan, Patrick M., Charles M. Tolbert II, and E. M. Beck. 1981. "The Circle Has No Close." *American Journal of Sociology* 86:887–94.

Houghland, James G., Jr. 1985. "Industrial Sectors and Economic Outcomes: Experiences of Former CETA Participants." *Social Science Quarterly* 66:903–15.

Howe, Irving, ed. 1984. *Alternatives: Proposals for America from the Democratic Left.* New York: Pantheon Books.

Huntington, Samuel P. 1976. "The Change to Change: Modernization, Development, and Politics." In *Comparative Modernization: A Reader*, edited by Cyril E. Black, 25–61. Perspectives on Modernization. New York: Free Press.

In These Times. 1986. "Editorial: Wealth Triumphs, We Lose." August 6–19, 14.

Kalleberg, Arne L., and Aage B. Sørensen. 1979. "The Sociology of Labor Markets." *Annual Review of Sociology* 5:351–79.

Kalleberg, Arne L., Michael Wallace, and Robert P. Althauser. 1981. "Economic Segmentation, Worker Power, and Income Inequality." *American Journal of Sociology* 87:651–83.

Karmin, Monroe W., with Linda K. Lanier, Ron Scherer, Jack A. Seamonds, and Michael Bosc. 1984. "High Tech: Blessing or Curse?" *U.S. News and World Report* 96 (January 16): 38–44.

Kaufman, Robert L., and Seymour Spilerman. 1982. "The Age Structures of Occupations and Jobs." *American Journal of Sociology* 87:827–51.

Kemp, Alice Abel, and E. M. Beck. 1981. "Female Underemployment in Urban Labor Markets." In *Sociological Perspectives on Labor Markets*, edited by Ivar E. Berg, 251–72. New York: Academic Press.

Kerr, Clark. 1954. "The Balkanization of Labor Markets." In *Labor Mobility and Economic Opportunity*, by Edward Wight Bakke, Philip M. Hauser, Gladys L. Palmer, Charles A. Myers, Dale Yoder, and Clark Kerr, 92–110. Cambridge: Technology Press of Massachusetts Institute of Technology; New York: Wiley.

Kerr, Clark, John T. Dunlop, Frederick H. Harbison, and Charles A. Myers. 1960. *Industrialism and Industrial Man: The Problems of Labor and Management in Economic Growth.* Cambridge, Mass.: Harvard University Press.

Kilborn, Peter T. 1986. "U.S. Whites 10 Times Wealthier than Blacks, Census Study Finds." *New York Times*, July 19, 1.

Lauer, Robert H. 1977. *Perspectives on Social Change.* 2d ed. Boston: Allyn and Bacon.

Longman, Phillip. 1982. "Taking America to the Cleaners." *Washington Monthly*, 14(9): 24–30.

Mandel, Ernest. 1969. *Late Capitalism*, translated by Joris De Bres. London: Verso Editions.

Miller, Herman P. 1965. "Lifetime Income and Economic Growth." *American Economic Review* 55:834–44.

Mills, C. Wright. 1959. *The Sociological Imagination.* London: Oxford University Press.

Moore, Wilbert E. 1979. *World Modernization: The Limits of Convergence.* New York: Elsevier.

————. 1963. *Social Change*. Foundations of Modern Sociology Series. Engelwood Cliffs, N.J.: Prentice-Hall.

Müller, Ronald E. 1977. "National Economic Growth and Stabilization Policy in the Age of Multinational Corporations: The Challenge of Our Postmarket Economy." In *U.S. Economic Growth from 1976 to 1986: Prospects, Problems, and Patterns*. Vol. 12, *Economic Growth in the International Context*, 35–79. Studies prepared for the use of the Joint Economic Committee, U.S. Congress, 95th Cong. 1st sess. Washington, D.C.: U.S. Government Printing Office.

Nussbaum, Bruce, with Kathleen Failla, Christopher S. Eklund, Alex Beam, James R. Norman, and Kathleen Deveny. 1986. "The End of Corporate Loyalty?" *Business Week*, August 4, 42–49.

O'Connell, James. 1976. "The Concept of Modernization." In *Comparative Modernization*, edited by Cyril E. Black, 13–24. New York: Free Press.

O'Connor, James. 1973. *The Fiscal Crisis of the State*. New York: St. Martin's Press.

Offe, Claus. 1985. *Disorganized Capitalism: Contemporary Transformations of Work and Politics*, edited by John Keane. Studies in Contemporary German Social Thought. Cambridge: MIT Press.

Offe, Claus, and Helmut Wiesenthal. 1980. "Two Logics of Collective Action: Theoretical Notes on Social Class and Organizational Form." In *Political Power and Social Theory*, edited by Maurice Zeitlin, vol. 1, 67–115. Greenwich, Conn.: JAI Press.

Olson, Laura Katz. 1982. *The Political Economy of Aging: The State, Private Powers, and Social Welfare*. New York: Columbia University Press.

Palmore, Erdman B., and Kenneth Manton. 1974. "Modernization and Status of the Aged: International Correlations." *Journal of Gerontology* 29:205–10.

Parkin, Frank. 1971. *Class Inequality and Political Order: Social Stratification in Capitalist and Communist Societies*. New York: Praeger.

Parsons, Talcott. 1960. *Structure and Process in Modern Societies*. Glencoe, Ill.: Free Press.

————. 1940. "An Analytic Approach to the Theory of Social Stratification." *American Journal of Sociology* 45:841–62.

Pearce, Diana. 1986. "Women and Children in Poverty." *Southern Changes* 8(1): 1–2, 16–20.

Pepper, Claude. "The Unemployment Crisis Facing Older Americans." In *The Unemployment Crisis Facing Older Americans*, 59–76. U.S. Congress, House Select Committee on Aging, 97th Cong. 2d sess. Comm. Pub. 97–367. Washington, D.C.: U.S. Government Printing Office.

Pfeffer, Jeffrey. 1977. "Toward an Examination of Stratification in Organizations." *Administrative Science Quarterly* 22:553–67.

Piore, Michael J. 1973. "Fragments of a 'Sociological' Theory of Wages." *American Economic Review* 63:377–84.

Piven, Frances Fox, and Richard A. Cloward. 1982. *The New Class War: Reagan's Attack on the Welfare State and Its Consequences*. New York: Pantheon Books.

Reich, Michael, David M. Gordon, and Richard C. Edwards. 1973. "A Theory of Labor Market Segmentation." *American Economic Review* 63:359–65.

Reskin, Barbara F., and Heidi I. Hartmann, eds. 1986. *Women's Work, Men's Work: Sex Segregation on the Job*. Washington, D. C.: National Academy Press.

Reuters News Service. 1986. "Auto Industry Evolving." *The Atlanta Journal and Constitution*, March 16, 4M.

Riley, Matilda White, Marilyn Johnson, and Anne Foner. 1972. *Aging and Society*. Vol. 3, *A Sociology of Age Stratification*. New York: Russell Sage Foundation.

Rosenfeld, Carl, and Scott Campbell Brown. 1979. "The Labor Force Status of Older Workers." *Monthly Labor Review* 102(11): 12–18.

Rosenfeld, Rachel A. 1983. "Sex Segregation and Sectors: An Analysis of Gender Differences in Returns from Employer Changes." *American Sociological Review* 48:637–55.

Rostow, Walt Whitman. 1960. *The Stages of Economic Growth: A Non-Communist Manifesto*. Cambridge, England: Cambridge University Press.

Ryder, Norman B. 1965. "The Cohort as a Concept in the Study of Social Change." *American Sociological Review* 30:843–61.

Shepherd, William G. 1982. "Causes of Increased Competition in the U. S. Economy, 1939–1980." *Review of Economics and Statistics* 64:613–26.

Singelmann, Joachim. 1978. *From Agriculture to Services: The Transformation of Industrial Employment*. Sage Library of Social Research, vol. 69. Beverly Hills, Calif.: Sage.

Smelser, Neil J. 1966. "The Modernization of Social Relations." In *Modernization: The Dynamics of Growth*, edited by Myron Weiner, 110–21. New York: Basic Books.

Spaeth, Joe L. 1985. "Job Power and Earnings." *American Sociological Review* 50:603–17.

Spilerman, Seymour. 1977. "Careers, Labor Market Structure, and Socioeconomic Achievement." *American Journal of Sociology* 83:551–93.

Squires, Gregory D. 1984. "Capital Mobility versus Upward Mobility: The Racially Discriminatory Consequences of Plant Closings and Corporate Relocations." In *Sunbelt/Snowbelt: Urban Development and Regional Restructuring*, edited by Larry Sawers and William K. Tabb, 152–62. New York: Oxford University Press.

Stanback, Thomas M., Peter Bearse, Thierry J. Noyelle, and Robert Karasek. 1981. *Services: The New Economy*. Conservation of Human Resources Series, no. 20. Montclair, N.J.: Allanheld, Osmun.

Stanback, Thomas M., Jr., and Thierry J. Noyelle. 1982. *Cities in Transition: Changing Job Structures in Atlanta, Denver, Buffalo, Phoenix, Columbus (Ohio), Nashville, Charlotte*. Totowa, N.J.: Allanheld, Osmun.

Stolzenberg, Ross M. 1978. "Bringing the Boss Back In: Employer Size, Employee Schooling, and Socioeconomic Achievement." *American Sociological Review* 43:813–28.

———. 1975. "Occupations, Labor Markets and the Process of Wage Attainment." *American Sociological Review* 40:645–65.

Sullivan, Teresa A. 1981. "Sociological Views on Labor Markets: Some Missed Opportunities and Neglected Directions." In *Sociological Perspectives on Labor Markets*, edited by Ivar E. Berg, 329–46. New York: Academic Press.

Summers, Gene F., Sharon D. Evans, Frank Clemente, E. M. Beck, and Jon Minkoff. 1976. *Industrial Invasion of Nonmetropolitan America: A Quarter Century of Experience*. Praeger Special Studies in U.S. Economic, Social, and Political Issues. New York: Praeger.

Sutton, Frank X. 1963. "Social Theory and Comparative Politics." In *Comparative Politics, A Reader*, edited by Harry Eckstein and David E. Apter, 67–81. New York: Free Press of Glencoe.

Taylor, Frederick Winslow. 1911. *The Principles of Scientific Management*. New York: Harper.

Thurow, Lester C. 1975. *Generating Inequality: Mechanisms of Distribution in the U.S. Economy*. New York: Basic Books.

Tolbert, Charles, M., II. 1982. "Industrial Segmentation and Men's Career Mobility." *American Sociological Review* 47:457–77.

Tolbert, Charles M., II., Patrick M. Horan, and E. M. Beck. 1980. "The Structure of Economic Segmentation: A Dual Economy Approach." *American Journal of Sociology* 85:1095–1116.

Touraine, Alain. 1971. *The Post-Industrial Society: Tomorrow's Social History: Classes, Conflicts, and Culture in the Programmed Society*, translated by Leonard F. X. Mayhew. New York: Random House.

Tumin, Melvin M. 1960. "Competing Status Systems." In *Labor Commitment and Social Change in Developing Areas*, edited by Wilbert E. Moore and Arnold S. Feldman, 277–90. New York: Social Science Research Council.

———. 1953. "Some Principles of Stratification: A Critical Analysis." *American Sociological Review* 18:387–94.

Urquhart, Michael. 1984. "The Employment Shift to Services: Where Did It Come From?" *Monthly Labor Review* 107(4):15–22.

U.S. Bureau of the Census. 1985. *Money Income and Poverty Status of Families and Persons in the United States: 1984*. Current Population Reports, ser. P-60. Consumer Income, no. 146. Washington, D.C.: U.S. Department of Commerce.

U.S. Congress. House. Select Committee on Aging. 1982. *The Unemployment Crisis Facing Older Americans*. 97th Cong. 2d sess. Comm. Pub. 97–367. Washington, D.C.: U.S. Government Printing Office.

U.S. Department of Labor. Bureau of Labor Statistics. 1986. "Current Labor Statistics." *Monthly Labor Review* 109(11).

———. 1985. *Handbook of Labor Statistics*. Bulletin 2217. Washington, D.C.: U.S. Government Printing Office.

———. 1980. *Handbook of Labor Statistics*. Bulletin 2070. Washington, D.C.: U.S. Government Printing Office.

———. 1973. *Handbook of Labor Statistics 1973*. Bulletin 1790. Washington, D.C.: U.S. Government Printing Office.

Vietorisz, Thomas, and Bennett Harrison. 1973. "Labor Market Segmentation: Positive Feedback and Divergent Development." *American Economic Review* 63: 366–76.

Walker, Alan. 1981. "Towards a Political Economy of Old Age." *Aging and Society* 1:73–94.

Wallace, Michael, and Arne L. Kalleberg. 1981. "Economic Organization of Firms and Labor Market Consequences: Toward a Specification of Dual Economy Theory." In *Sociological Perspectives on Labor Markets*, edited by Ivar E. Berg, 77–117. New York: Academic Press.

Welch, Finis. 1979. "Effects of Cohort Size on Earnings: The Baby Boom Babies' Financial Bust." *Journal of Political Economy* 87:S65–S97.

Wernick, Murray S., and James L. McIntire. 1980. "Employment and Labor Force Growth: Recent Trends and Future Prospects." In *Special Study on Economic Change*. Vol. 1, *Human Resources and Demographics: Characteristics of People and Policy*, 101–52. Studies prepared for the use of the special study on economic change of the Joint Economic Committee, U.S. Congress 96th Cong. 2d sess. Washington, D.C.: U.S. Government Printing Office.

Wilcock, Richard C., and Walter H. Franke. 1963. *Unwanted Workers: Permanent Layoffs and Long-Term Unemployment*. New York: Free Press of Glencoe.

Wilkinson, Frank. 1981. "Preface." In *The Dynamics of Labour Market Segmentation*, edited by Frank Wilkinson, vii–xii. London: Academic Press.

Williams, Lena. 1986. "Older U.S. Women Found Struggling." *New York Times*, May 8, 16.

Winter, Ralph E. 1984. "New Givebacks. Even Profitable Firms Press Workers to Take Permanent Pay Cuts." *Wall Street Journal*, March 6, 1.

Wright, Erik Olin. 1978. "Race, Class and Income Inequality." *American Journal of Sociology* 83:1368–97.

Wright, Erik Olin, and Luca Perrone. 1977. "Marxist Class Categories and Income Inequality." *American Sociological Review* 42:32–55.

Wright, Erik Olin, and Joachim Singelmann. 1982. "Proletarianization in the Changing American Class Structure." In *Marxist Inquiries: Studies of Labor, Class, and States*, edited by Michael Burawoy and Theda Skocpol, S176–S209. Chicago: University of Chicago Press.

Young, Anne McDougall, and Howard Hayghe. 1984. "More U.S. Workers Are College Graduates." *Monthly Labor Review* 107 (3): 46–49.

Zucker, Lynne G., and Carolyn Rosenstein. 1981. "Taxonomies of Institutional Structure: Dual Economy Reconsidered." *American Sociological Review* 46: 869–84.

Index

About the Author

LEANN M. TIGGES is a postdoctoral fellow at the Carolina Population Center at the University of North Carolina at Chapel Hill.

Dr. Tigges has conducted research on a variety of issues of economic transformation and social stratification. Her current research interests include rural industrialization, poverty, women's employment, and regional change. She is the author of articles on the South and on sectoral change.

Dr. Tigges received her Ph.D. in sociology from the University of Missouri (Columbia) in 1984.